HAUNTED WEBSTER GROVES

Legends and Firsthand Accounts of
Ghosts in Webster Groves, Missouri

PATRICK DORSEY

FACTUAL PLANET

ST. LOUIS

ISBN 978-1-939437-34-1

Cover Illustration by Evan Willnow
Copyright © 2015 by Legendary Planet, LLC

Edited by Lori Callander

Book design by Evan Willnow

Typeset in Alegreya and Immortal

Manufactured in the United States of America

Factual Planet is an imprint of
Legendary Planet, LLC
PO Box 440081
Saint Louis, Missouri 63144-0081

LegendaryPlanet.com

Table of Contents

Why the Big Margin?

Factual Planet books are designed to promote reader involvement and encourage the reader to get the most from the text.

To that end, all Factual Planet books employ an exceptionally wide margin on the outside edge of each page. Known in book design as a *scholar's margin*, it gives readers space to make notes on a page as they read. (No more cramming thoughts around the author's name and the page numbers or showers of sticky notes falling out!)

So, please, take your favorite pen or pencil and make use of the space provided for your own comments, thoughts, and questions about the text presented.

Introduction

I was forewarned when I set out to write *Haunted Webster Groves*—Jim Longo, an old family friend and author of the *Haunted Odyssey* series of true ghostly stories told me, "Once you start looking for the spirits, *they'll* find *you*."

He was right. One afternoon, on a lark, I posted on a local Webster Groves Facebook page, asking for residents to share their haunted stories. I got nearly a dozen responses to follow up with—in just the first ninety minutes! Soon after that, people who I already knew, who had never before said a word about ghosts or hauntings, began contacting me with stories of their experiences with the supernatural.

Almost everyone loves a good ghost story. Even the perpetually frightened can appreciate a tale of someone long-dead keeping an eye out for loved ones left behind, while unbelievers can still delight in a ghost story for its connections to history or just on its merits as a story. Some enjoy the thrill, some enjoy the escape from the everyday, some enjoy among the chills the reassurance that there's an existence beyond this one. Whatever the reason, in nearly every culture around the world, human beings have been recounting stories of the unquiet dead for as long as they've been able to gather to share them. And those stories that purport to be true ... those always hold even more interest.

Why Webster Groves?

First, as a resident of Webster Groves, there's the obvious "Wow … right around the corner? Right up the street? Right *next door?*" aspect of finding and listening to the tales of ghosts and hauntings in your own neighborhood. So, living here in Webster Groves nearly my entire adult life, inquiring of my neighbors or the other school parents was an intriguing and uncomplicated way to unearth and gather stories—Webster Groves is, as celebrated author and Webster Groves native Jonathan Franzen called it, a "friendly, unpretentious town." People here were eager to step up when I began this effort, and they required little prodding to share their experiences or point a hapless writer to someone else who had told them a fantastic, ghostly tale.

Further, with blocks dotted with houses proudly bearing "Century Home" plaques that indicate they're a hundred years old or more (just over five percent of the buildings in Webster Groves are over a hundred years old, with two structures that are two hundred years old), Webster Groves is a community where its history is still standing in brick, plaster, and wood. Combine that with generations of residents choosing to live in the town where they grew up, and Webster Groves has the kind of long history that makes it a natural place to find stories of ghosts and hauntings.

The city's story goes back to 1802, when the area was still known to the Osage and Dakota Indians and to European fur trappers as Dry Ridge. As a buttress against the influence of the English, the Spanish government was issuing land grants to promote French land ownership while the entire region transitioned from Spanish to French rule. French national Gregorie Sarpy, who had married into St. Louis' prominent Chouteau family, was granted 6,002 acres by the last Spanish colonial governor of the region, Charles de Hautte Delassus. This acreage included most of what would become Webster Groves.

Nineteenth century overcrowding, as well as awful summer heat along the Mississippi River and unhealthy conditions, led to several cholera epidemics. The conditions pushed people from the City of St. Louis to the cleaner and more peaceful communities edging the city's outskirts. Communities sprang up around the Pacific Railroad line, offering quiet country neighborhoods with single-family houses and an easy commute into the city—the beginnings of the commuter suburb, an institution that still defines the St. Louis region today.

Following the Civil War, the area saw further growth as returning soldiers settled. Building homes and businesses, churches and schools, they created communities where they could raise their families and live and prosper. These communities pushed in all directions as they grew. In 1896 five—Webster, Webster Park, Old Orchard, Selma, and Tuxedo Park—merged to become the City of Webster Groves, employing the motto "A Great Place to Live, Work and Play" that is used by the city to this day.

A history that reaches back to colonial times? People escaping the filth, disease, and corruption of nineteenth century cities? The Civil War? Homes and businesses standing and occupied, some for over a century, witnessing silently the lives lived and passed within their walls? Practically a recipe for ghost stories, I thought.

And I was right.

Legends and Firsthand Accounts

Our stories define us, and stories define our community as well. They entertain us and connect us to the past, helping us reflect on the bygone while pondering what may be. Collecting these stories of ghosts and hauntings captures history—not just of Webster Groves as a city, but as a community of people.

I'm a storyteller and writer, not a ghost hunter. So, first and foremost, *Haunted Webster Groves* is a collection of stories. These are accounts and events set down just as they were told to me. I performed no TV-style night vision camera investigations of the locations discussed, and I didn't research the homes or buildings to unearth some bit of arcane history to verify or refute the various storytellers' accounts. What was important to me in gathering these was to capture the experiences the people here reported having. They shared with me stories of sounds that unsettled them, smells that disturbed them, visions that surprised and even terrified them—experiences they chose to discuss with me and have now added to the history of Webster Groves through this book. I found each story included here credible, convincing, and compelling as it was told to me, and I have no reason to doubt the sincerity of any of the tellers.

One very important element of relating these people's experiences is maintaining their privacy. The stories included here are events from their lives that they were gracious enough to share—some hesitantly, for reasons ranging from fear of ridicule to concern over uninvited gawkers. Except for the very public places like Webster

University or the Theatre Guild of Webster Groves, identities have been obscured for good reason. Enjoy the stories in *Haunted Webster Groves*. Consider them and discuss them with your friends. But keep in mind that these are people's lives and homes, and please don't hunt them out for interviews, drop by with questions, or trespass in the middle of the night hoping to glimpse something otherworldly.

Haunted Webster Groves is made up of two parts, each reflecting the main species of stories I encountered.

Legends contains the stories of hauntings that are well-known, the ones have been recounted in other books and have become famous. For these, I've included information that has already been reported, but I've also made every effort to seek out people who have experienced the happenings personally so I can share the stories of the locations as they were told to me.

Firsthand Accounts comprises the stories shared with me by people I knew from the neighborhood or my kids' schools, or by someone the neighbors or PTO parents pointed me to, or who volunteered their stories as word of this project spread. These were the real "right next door" stories that raised a shiver along the spine as a homeowner revealed creepy or preternatural details of an encounter with the unearthly, practically in my own back yard.

It was an amazing and spine-chilling journey drawing together these stories of the ghostly from my own neighborhoods in Webster Groves. I can only hope you thrill at reading them as much as I did unearthing them.

Patrick Dorsey
Webster Groves
October, 2015

Legends

North Gore Avenue –
The Rock House,
Great Circle/Edgewood
Children's Center

When St. Louis' first great cholera epidemic left a troubling—and growing—number of orphaned children homeless on the city's streets, the St. Louis Association for the Relief of Orphaned Children was formed in 1834 to help. After years of providing aid and support, their city-based St. Louis Protestant Orphan Asylum became increasingly unsuitable for the children in their care. In 1859, the association purchased a shuttered seminary, the Rock House, and its surrounding land. They relocated their facilities and their charges to the countryside that would soon become Webster Groves. In 1943, the facility was renamed the Edgewood Children's Center and became part of Great Circle in 2009. Over the years, its mission expanded to include treatment and support for disruptive and emotionally troubled children and its campus grew to include several more modern buildings along with the Rock House.

Certainly born of a dedication to providing help, with such a long history and the troubled nature of the children who need it, the Rock House has its share of hauntings.

Stories tell of a hidden tunnel beneath the building that was used for hiding and protecting slaves in pre-Civil War days. They say in 1890, two children died playing in the tunnel after losing their way. A 1910 fire gutted the old building and claimed the life of at least one child under care there. Some say the children lost in both these tragedies haunt the Rock House today.

THE GIRL WALKING THE GROUNDS

A——, a successful Webster Groves realtor, reached out to me with his own experience at the Rock House. "This was back around 1979. I was on the night shift at the Edgewood Children's Home. I was new and not familiar with any stories whatsoever.

"This was the overnight shift, 11:00 p.m. to 7:00 a.m., and I had just checked in. They wanted us to do rounds with a big, long flashlight. We'd go outside and just walk around the buildings, counter-clockwise, and you'd end up at the Rock House, and then you'd go back to where your little station was.

"It was one of those snowy nights, where it's kind of misty and the snow's blowing around. It was maybe one o'clock and I'd rounded the corner of the girls' cottage and I saw a little girl down the hill. She was standing by the corner of the school. It was south, about twenty yards from the Rock House. She was quite a distance away. I saw her sitting in what I thought at that distance was a white nightgown. And it was *cold* outside.

"I didn't shine the light on her because I didn't want to scare her. I walked quietly up to her, with the flashlight pointed down at the ground. When I got up to her, maybe fifteen or twenty feet away, I said, 'Hey, sweetie,' and she ducked around the corner and I couldn't see her anymore.

"I shined the flashlight around that corner, and my hair started to stand on end. I don't know what I was picking up, but it just felt weird. I saw the back of her as she was running, and then she was sitting on the steps of the Rock House. I shined the flashlight on my chest, to light me up without looking too spooky, and said, 'Hi! My name's A——. Honey, you need to get inside.' I was just talking to her like a guy would who's trying to help a little girl out in the cold at one o'clock in the morning. When I got up to her, maybe another ten or twenty feet, she just whisped away, like smoke."

A—— threw his hands up and shook his head, still flabbergasted by what he saw that long-ago night. "I stood there for a moment. I didn't know what I just saw. At first I thought it was the wind, and I had glasses and maybe they just got all foggy... I worked up all kinds of excuses for what I saw. And then I realized that one of the girls must be missing.

"So I did a bedroom check and counted all the girls and looked at their log and talked to their night shift staff, and all the girls were where they were supposed to be. And I went over to the boys', thinking maybe it's a new boy and he was maybe in a white t-shirt. And I looked at the log and there's no boys missing.

"I realized then I had to put this in the log. And I'm the new guy! So I started thinking and playing it back in my mind to make sure I had everything exactly, and I wrote it all down.

"So, in the morning the next guy came in to relieve me. He read the log and said, 'Wow! You met the Rock House ghost!' And then he told me all of his stories and some from a few others he knew. They were all really cavalier about it, like 'Ah, big deal. It happens.'"

STRANGE THINGS IN THE ATTIC

K——, another former employee, worked on the top floor of the Rock House, often late into the night and often alone. Or at least the only *human being* there in the small, dark hours. "There were no elevators, only steps. With my job, I was often the last one in the building, and I'd hear little thumps in the night." She conceded that, maybe, it was just an old building creaking, or simply squirrels on the roof.

"Perhaps," she said. "But the microwave on our floor would turn on randomly. And when we'd hear it start and go over to turn it off, the timer wouldn't be counting down. The microwave would just be on and running. Same thing with the coffee pot and the fans. They'd go on by themselves, and when you'd go to turn them off, you'd find them with their switches in the "on" position—physically switched on.

"When I was working alone, late, I would sometimes hear someone walking up and down the 'steps. I'd check the stairs and there'd be no one. Sometimes, I'd hear knocking, like from inside the walls.

"Up in the attic, on the top floor where we worked, the walls were lined with these short, three-foot high doors. They were used at one time as storage lockers for the children. I would sometimes hear scratching from behind the doors." Though creepy and certainly something included in many stories of hauntings, I was curious why she was sure the scratching wasn't from something ordinary in an old building, like mice. "I'd open the doors and check. They were completely clean. If there were mice, there would be little debris, droppings. There were no signs of any mice at all.

"I can tell you about someone else's experience there. In the front entry foyer on the main level, they had one of those curved mirrors for seeing around corners. They used it for keeping an eye on things on the first floor. The receptionist told me that, late at night one night, he heard someone coming in through the back door of the building. So he looked in the mirror to see who it was and saw the door open and close ... with no one there. I also used to talk with the custodian—he used to work after hours—and he said he used to hear a ball bouncing on the floor at night."

Edgar Road –
The Loretto-Hilton Center
for the Performing Arts

A ctors, it seems, are the only thing found in theatres
more than ghosts. Perhaps because of the often
long history of many theatre buildings, perhaps because
of the intense emotion that plays out on stage night
after night and year after year, perhaps because of the
colorful imaginations of the creative talents that stage
those shows, the tradition of theatre hauntings is both
rich and commonplace. Pick almost any theatre, from
the oldest of London or Paris to the grandest of Broadway
to the smallest backwater hall, and with only a few
questions, you can usually unearth someone's account of
the unexplained or ghostly.

The Loretto-Hilton Center is no exception.

Located on the campus of Webster University, the
Loretto-Hilton Center for the Performing Arts was
founded in 1966 by Jacqueline Grennan Wexler and Marita
Michenfelder Woodruff, a pair of Sisters of Loretto nuns
who dreamed of a respectable venue where the students
of their college's theatre department could work and learn
among theatre professionals.

Funded mainly through a $1.5 million gift from hotel
mogul Conrad Hilton, the Loretto-Hilton's space was
designed to be convertible. With retractable walls, it can
be configured as a classroom, chapel, theatre, or concert
hall, with a capacity that can be adjusted from 499 to 1200.
The facility is home to The Repertory Theatre of St. Louis
("The Rep" as it's called) and the Opera Theatre of St. Louis,
as well as Webster University's Conservatory of Theatre &

Dance. An award-winning venue, the Loretto-Hilton has staged both entertaining and acclaimed performances through the years, and continues strong today.

And like many long-running theatres, the students, staff, actors, and crew there have experienced a wide range of ghostly encounters. Most of the experiences have been of the typical variety, with reports of knocks and thumps and shaking doors with no one on the other side. One recent example of this occurred in 2014. During intermission at a preview of *A Midsummer Night's Dream* when Marketing and Artistic Director Steve Woolf heard a crash, like a light dropping up on the catwalk—only no one was there. Becky Hadley, the Rep's Public Relations Manager at the time, heard the same crash during the opening night performance.

But there are stories about another spirit haunting the theatre, one known for the help and assistance he's offered the theatre's crew both in life and after.

Peter Sargent, the Dean of Webster University's Leigh Gerdine College of Fine Arts, has been with the Loretto-Hilton and the Rep literally from the first day in 1966, so it's no exaggeration to say he has seen everything that's gone on there. When I started inquiring about the ghosts at the theatre, everyone I spoke to said the same thing: *Go talk to Peter—he knows all the stories.*

Peter laughed when I mentioned that universal recommendation "I wouldn't say *all* the stories..."

But he does know the stories of the theatre's ghosts.

"As far as we can tell," Peter told me, "there are two ghosts in the Loretto-Hilton Center. One was a construction worker who, in 1965, at the time construction of the building was underway, fell off the back wall as they were doing work—maybe bricklaying—and the lore is, whenever anyone involved in the construction of a theatre passes away during the job, their spirit remains there.

"Although I haven't met that person, we believe he does occupy some of the lower levels of the theatre. Weirdly, I was just in a conversation recently with someone in the construction business who knew the fellow at the time it happened.

"Our second regular visitor to the theatre is a guy named David Hitzer. David was Master Electrician for the Rep and worked regularly in the theatre. Amongst other things he did, he ran the Backstage Club when he was on campus. One year—I think it was 1982, while we were in tech rehearsal for a Rep production of *Tartuffe*—David had come to rehearsal after the end of the Muny* season, where he had just done the end-of-season strike. He came almost directly to our tech rehearsal and he wasn't feeling all that well. So he left the students on the light board that afternoon and went to take a nap.

"He never woke up from that nap.

"He was up on the catwalk when that shockingly occurred. But I'm pretty well convinced, from a variety of elements, that David never left the building. There's never been an actual sighting of him—"

Somehow fitting for a backstage crew guy.

"—But there are two things David is protective of: the focus of the lights and their operation, and the inherent safety of the students.

"He apparently has gone around and checked and the improved on the lighting for shows—the focus and the arrangement of the lighting. We know there have been adjustments made, *improvements*. The lights weren't moved, but they were aimed differently, and nobody would own up to the tinkering. It always happens late at night, and can only be attributed to David."

*Better known as The Muny, the Municipal Theatre Association of St. Louis is the famous permanent outdoor theatre venue located in St. Louis' Forest Park.

Peter considered a moment, then continued, "There are also three instances I can think of where a student on the catwalk lost their balance and felt that they were about to fall, but was then miraculously pulled back and saved from a dangerous drop. Each one said they felt a hand grab a shoulder or belt and pull them back. There's a feeling that David is around to help protect students and provide that kind of safety up on the catwalks.

"He worked with the Rep and the students here for at least a decade. He was an icon in working here. He was a passionate person about being part of all this. And I'm pretty certain he was the kind of person who'd say, 'Damned if I'm going to leave!'"

Plant Avenue –
The Gehm House

It's perhaps the most famous haunting in Webster Groves. The story of the Gehm House on Plant Avenue has been chronicled in books from Hans Holzer's well-known *Ghosts: True Encounters with the World Beyond* to James Longo's well-respected *Haunted Odyssey: Ghostly Tales of the Mississippi Valley*.

What's generally known is: The two-story, wood-and-brick house was built by Bart Adams as a summer retreat sometime around 1890. It's known by the name of its second occupant, Henry Gehm, an eccentric railroad businessman whose company built the first gondola cars. He was said to be distrustful of banks following the stock market crash of 1929, and rumor held he buried his money in gold on his property. He lived in the house from 1906 to 1944 before passing away from cancer.

FIRST REPORTS: THE FURRY FAMILY

In 1956, S.L. Furry, his wife Fannie, and their children moved in to the house on Plant Avenue. Almost immediately, Fannie Furry began experiencing strange and unexplainable happenings in their new home. It began in the middle of the night, at exactly three o'clock one morning, when Fannie felt someone shaking her awake—yet she found no one was touching her. This went on night after night, at precisely the same time.

One night, she was startled from her sleep by an earsplitting hammering on the headboard of her bed. Turning on the light and expecting to find shattered, splintered wood, she could detect not even as a mark on the headboard.

At other times, she heard pounding on the bedroom windows and the sounds of footsteps on the stairs, never finding anyone there who could be responsible for the disturbance. One morning, she came downstairs and discovered a wall sconce that had been firmly mounted to the wall unfastened and lying on the floor.

Although he, too experienced some of the strange occurrences, her husband was skeptical ... until he awoke in the middle of the night and watched a white, misty silhouette float down the hall and pass through the door of his daughter's bedroom. When, after several years of odd happenings, their youngest daughter began telling them of the strange little boy who was visiting her—accompanied by an old woman in a black dress who would spank her with a broom— the Furrys decided to move out.

THE WALSHES MOVE IN

After living nine years with the unusual activity, the Furrys moved to a new house—still in Webster Groves—and the Walsh family took up residence, renting the Plant Avenue House and moving in with their two youngest daughters.

It wasn't long before they, too, were experiencing the out-of-the-ordinary.

While making dinner one night, mother Clare Walsh found the family dog cowering in a corner of the kitchen. Immediately concerned for their pet, she glanced around and realized the dog was keeping an eye on a faint, hazy figure in the doorway. She watched the shimmering apparition glide into the living room and then vanish. Soon after, the Walshes began to hear footsteps climbing up and down the stairs at night, just as the Furrys experienced.

THE ACTIVITY GOES FURTHER

The Walshes, though, experienced more activity than the Furrys. Lights turned on and off by themselves, and a typewriter in their daughter's room could be heard typing with no one near it. Drawers were frequently found open, their contents strewn all over the floor. While doing laundry, Clare Walsh witnessed a sweater snatched into the air and then lowered slowly to the floor by unseen hands.

Increasingly, the attic became the focus of the unexplained activity in the house. They soon found their attic door refused to stay shut. Night after night the family secured it, and morning after morning they found it standing wide open—Clare once even listened to it open and close four times in the middle of the night. Furniture and toys stored in the attic were regularly found repositioned, including a large chest of drawers that was shifted from one wall to another, a large trunk that was pulled out and set in the center of the room, and a doll's house that was relocated from a high shelf to a lower one.

Interviewing her neighbors about the street in general and her house in particular, Clare heard tell of Henry Gehm's treasure-hiding. Recalling the activity on the attic stairs, she searched there and found one of the treads was made to lift off, revealing a small hiding place beneath. It was empty, but with her discovery, she began to consider that their unseen visitor was Mr. Gehm himself, returning to check up on his buried fortune.

She had this theory perhaps confirmed when what she believed was Henry Gehm's spirit appeared to her. He directed her to the attic and a concealed doorway that hid a secret chamber. Unfortunately, like the hiding place in the stairs, the chamber was empty and whatever mystery the ghost was leading her to remained unsolved.

Finally, all the mysterious activity got to be too much for the Walshes, and they decided to move—into a newly built house, one never lived in by anyone else before, and therefore, presumably free of any hauntings. Almost as a reminder, on their last day on Plant Avenue, the Walshes again heard the footsteps on the stairs.

THE MOST RECENT EXPERIENCES

Soon after, the house became the property of the V—— family, who have lived there ever since. Thanks to too many years of Sherlock Holmes and Philip Marlowe books and *Banacek* and *Law & Order* reruns, I was able to track down C——, who raised his family in the notorious house on Plant Avenue. They experienced much of the same activity as the owners of the house before them, including hazy figures, being awakened by violent bed-shaking, a family dog troubled by something unseen, bedding being yanked away, and noises from the empty attic. But C——'s perspective after decades in the most notorious haunted house in Webster Groves ... well, it was intriguing, and led to an afternoon discussion that was thoughtful and thought-provoking but not at all what I expected.

VISITING THE HAUNTED HOUSE

If you squinted, the house could certainly pass for a classic haunted house. Hidden in part by the thick branches of huge, old, Webster Groves trees, the three-story wooden frame house was well-tended but clearly very old. Its windows were those wide, open-looking windows of an old house, the kind that make you think you've spotted a silhouette or shape in them—mostly because you're expecting to.

Under the hollow gaze of those windows, I climbed the weathered wood steps to the front porch and rang the doorbell. After only a moment, a slender, elderly gentleman answered the door. C—— was of course expecting me. I introduced myself and he shook my hand with a firm grip and invited me in.

The living room was good-sized, neat and uncluttered, with a certain Asian bent to the décor. C—— offered me a seat on the couch and then lowered himself to sit at its opposite end.

"This particular house is probably the most famous of the haunted houses in Webster Groves," he began. "It was Hans Holzer's publication that started the notoriety of this house, back around 1970.* Most of the subsequent publications simply rehashed what Holzer had come up with.

"When I got your message, it triggered in me a desire that I had to write about what happens to famous old haunted houses." He had explained in our correspondence before the interview that friends and family had experienced many ghostly happenings in the house. But with his background in the physical sciences, he could usually find possible natural causes for most of what they reported. And that, interestingly, as he and his wife started discouraging the notoriety of the house, ghostly phenomena decreased. He mentioned he had theories on why that was.

A haunted house whose activity actually decreased over time, at the effort of the homeowner ... the very idea ran contrary to every ghost story or scary movie I knew, fictional or not.

C—— recounted for me how he'd come to own the house. A Webster Groves resident as a child, he was retiring after twenty years of military service and he and his wife were looking for a place to settle down, a "permanent home" as he referred to it. "I had friends living in Webster Groves

*Holzer's GOTHIC GHOSTS (1972)

27

and they told us about a house that had been on the market, and then taken off the market. They thought the reason it had been taken off the market was that it wasn't being sold. And the reason they thought it wasn't being sold was because of this book. My friend showed me the book, and of course, it was Hans Holzer's book, which featured a story about this house in Webster Groves..."

They found the house appealing, but not just for its Webster charm. Planning to study psychology as the beginning of his next career, he considered, "What could be a better place to live for someone investigating psychology than in a haunted house? An *authenticated* haunted house," he added with a wink, "bona fide by Hans Holzer!

"We had three children. It was very interesting the first few years. My younger son had a lot of ghostly experiences in the house. And my wife has stories... There was one time, I was away and my wife was in bed, and she felt someone *tuck her in*—someone pushing in the edges of the bedding all around her! She used to tell amazing ghost stories. But she doesn't tell them anymore. They represent something in the past for her, something that is no more as the activity has died down.

"The media back then ... we had TV people coming, wanting to do programs here once they found out somebody was occupying the famous Plant Avenue House on a permanent basis. And there were curiosity seekers. And friends. So my family, particularly the kids and their friends, had a lot of ghostly experiences in the house. And I had some too. For me, it was mostly 'bump in the night' experiences. And with my background in the physical sciences, I could usually find alternate explanations for anything that occurred.

"The notoriety, the people coming in—that got to be a little bit much. As a matter of fact, there was one afternoon, close to Halloween—"

Naturally...

"—there was a knock at the door. I opened it, and there were two little kids, a boy and a girl, probably about ten years old. They asked, 'Can we come in and look at your fireplace?' And I said, 'Why, no! Why do you want to look at my fireplace?' 'Well,' they said, 'our teacher told us at that at about this time of the year, there's a spirit that comes back here looking for gold that he stored in the fireplace.' Now, I had never heard that story—I had a lot of stories about the house, but not that one. So I said, 'Sure! Come on in!'"

He swayed to his feet and led me across the room to the old living room hearth. "We went over to this fireplace. And we looked at the back, and sure enough, there was a loose brick! I pulled the brick out, and there *was* a cavity back behind it. Now, there wasn't any gold in there, but it was obvious that it had been a storage spot. Since then, because of the building code, I cemented this up."

His thin finger traced near the back wall of the fireplace. Almost uniformly blackened by decades of soot, I could make out the pale gray of the repair.

THE THEORY, AND EVERYTHING

"But the point is, all of these experiences, because of the notoriety of the house, got to be a little too much. So we started pushing them aside. And that was when the phenomena decreased.

"Now, why was that? Was it because we were trying to tone down the notoriety and get rid of them? Or was it because we changed our attitudes about the ghosts, and we didn't allow the curiosity seekers that believed firmly in them to come in? Maybe that's the reason they died out."

We talked for over an hour, our discussion ranging from philosophy and physics to psychology and chemistry, all the fields of study C—— had taken up through the years in order to reach understanding in general of the world around him and in particular the haunted house he lived in. We talked of religion, the basis for belief and the human need for it. Names like Schrodinger and Heisenberg and Fromm flew alongside Maslow, Jung, Radin and Tart. It was a fascinating back-and-forth that literally reached from the essence of infinity to the nature of the sub-atomic particle, touching on humankind's limitations in viewing those edges and the theories on the effect our own observations have in not just defining them, but literally making them what they are.

"As you can see I believe all things are *possible* with my experiences of almost eighty-seven years kicking around. I believe in ghosts, I believe in spirits. I believe in everything. And through many studies of the physical sciences and the social sciences, too—particularly psychology—I've developed a tentative hypothesis that anything is possible but we have to live in the here and now and deal with what is probable."

So, I echoed back to him, the change in expectations has led to the decline in activity?

"Expectations is one *possible* reason it's declined. Another is that it wasn't valid phenomena in the first place. A third is that the ghosts have given up on us.

"My expectations have not changed. It's not because of my skepticism that the ghostly activity's dwindled. There is nothing that would thrill me more than to shake hands with old Mr. Gehm.

"As far as I can see," he continued, "two things happen: Haunted houses just die out—like old soldiers, they fade away. Or, they get taken over commercially and become a public enterprise."

My thoughts went to the Sorrell-Weed House in Savannah, Georgia, or even St. Louis' own Lemp Mansion. Both are places known for being haunted that have literally capitalized on their spectral notoriety with tours and activities for the curious.

"In this house, we have very carefully avoided commercialization. And as the stories fade out, I've been left to consider whether they have faded out because of our desire to suppress them, or whether it's just because the people—we ourselves and others associated with us—have sort of gotten away from the *idea* of the ghosts, and changed the perception."

A Look Around

"As a matter of fact, I've got a collection... With my kids growing up here, going to school here, over the years, a lot of students wanted to write stories about this house. You know, for an assignment. So, I would usually say, 'Okay, sure, you can interview me, write what you want—as long as you give me a copy of it."

I laughed. As a writer and storyteller myself, the idea of someone gathering and keeping all the haunted house stories he was interviewed for over the years was utterly marvelous to me.

"So I have a collection," C—— continued, "Not just from school kids, but from Webster University over here." He no doubt noted my wide grin at that point. "Would you like to see them?

Of course!

He told me they were in his office upstairs. He led me to the staircase, and I got to climb the legendary haunted stairs I'd read about, where mysterious footsteps of unseen feet had been heard for decades.

On the second floor landing, C—— paused. He bent down, asking me if I was familiar with Clare Walsh's story of the stair tread with the secret hiding place beneath it. With a couple raps of his fist, he knocked the tread before him loose, revealing a small compartment.

"My kids used to like hiding their toys in here," he told me with a wink.

"Now, the family that lived here the longest was the Gehm family. They had two children, Julie and Harry. And both of them have come to visit us. I got out of them *their* stories about the house."

But everything I'd read said the activity began *after* Mr. Gehm's death.

"Oh, they were very incensed about that, and that things were made to sound more mysterious than they were. For example, I showed this compartment to Julie Gehm, and she said it wasn't a great secret: 'That's where my parents used to hide the silverware whenever we left the house for vacation or a trip,' she said."

After he replaced the tread, we pressed on. Nearing the very top of the stairs, it occurred to me that we were now heading to the infamous attic of Clare Walsh's stories. As I joined him on the top floor, C—— stopped and turned, pointing at the middle of the wall. "When I bought the house, there was a bathtub right here."

Just setting at the very top of the steps?

"This was the bedroom for the housekeeper," he explained. He told me of an investigation they'd had at the house, where one of the psychics on the team claimed to have isolated a spirit—or entity, as they referred to it—by the name of Wilma, who had been the housekeeper here for the house's original owner, Bart Adams. "I was trying to get the psychics to contact Wilma and get her to help clean up the house now!" he joked, then added in a low voice, "My wife gets mad when I tell that story."

THE TREASURE

C—— paused and indicated the wall to his left. "I think it was in one of Hans Holzer's books he talked about an attic door that wouldn't stay shut? Well, here it is—and, look! It's open!" His eyes sprang wide in mock surprise.

Looking over the simple door, cracked open for a glimpse at the small reach-in closet, I suggested drily perhaps *unlatched* was a better description than *open*. He pushed on the back panel and I could see what had been portrayed before as a secret chamber behind a hidden panel. It looked to me like ... more closet.

"This door ... when I had Julie Gehm up here, I showed her the panel and she said, 'Oh, yeah, back in there's where father used to keep his moonshine!'"

A real treasure when the Gehms lived there—back during Prohibition.

He showed me through the space that had once been the mysterious attic where Clare Walsh had heard footsteps, found furniture and large toys rearranged, and faced the apparition that led her to the hidden doorway and secret chamber. Now, it was a retreat to be envied by any author or thinker, quiet and removed from the rest of the house. The ceiling was sloped to follow the pitch of the roof immediately above. Sunlight spilled in through the banks of windows lining the walls and from a skylight in the ceiling. And in the middle of it all, a cluttered desk was ringed by crammed bookcases. C—— reached into one, withdrawing a handful of books and a thick folder.

I recognized the first book as he handed it to me. "Now, you said you've read Holzer. How about these others?" He passed me Robbi Courtaway's *Spirits of St. Louis* and Jim Longo's *Haunted Odyssey* and then Troy Taylor's *Haunted St. Louis*. A few I owned; all I'd read.

He laid the folder down on the desk and opened it, revealing a neat stack of crisply folded papers. Some were plain copy paper, others yellowing newspaper clippings. The first headline I spied began, "The Unspeakable Horror..." C—— smiled sheepishly as I laughed at the delightfully lurid title. As he continued paging through the folder, I identified the layouts and typefaces of the old St. Louis *Post-Dispatch* from the 1970s. One page he unfolded proudly: a letter to the editor he'd penned years ago. In it, as the owner and occupant of one of the area's most noted haunted houses, he refuted with tongue firmly in cheek a then-recent *Post-Dispatch* article bemoaning the lack of "respectable" ghosts in St. Louis.

Continuing to dig through the stack, we found more pieces, from the Webster Groves High School *Echo* to the Webster University school newspaper to the *Java Journal*. But the best were the folded, typed pages, with dates going back decades. Some were from Webster Groves grade schools such as Edgar Road, some were by students from the high school just a few blocks over, with teachers' comments and grades scrawled in the margins.

A wonderful collection of pieces, it showed not just the reach of the house's legend, but the care C——had devoted to cataloging them to better study and fathom them as he continued in his quest to understand the human place, the human role, in the vastness of Creation. I realized then, in spite of the rumors and legends and the searches others had made through the years for gold there, what was laid out on the table before us was the Plant Avenue House's genuine treasure.

Lockwood Avenue –
Loretto Hall, Webster University

In a long, dark habit and almost hooded in a black veil, a nun can be an imposing figure. A silent, shadowy, ghostly nun floating just above the floor, then, can be downright alarming—as students and staff at Webster University in Webster Groves can attest.

Like the community where it's situated, Webster University has a long, vibrant history. Its cornerstone was laid in 1915 by the Sisters of Loretto. A Catholic religious organization that was founded in 1812 to educate poor children on the frontier, its mission later expanded to provide education to any who might not otherwise receive it. Originally called Loretto College, the school's name was changed to Webster College in 1924. It was one of the first institutions west of the Mississippi to offer higher learning to women, becoming coeducational and admitting men in the 1960s. Renamed Webster University in 1983, the school has been a pioneer in non-traditional and alternative programs for working adults and military personnel, leading the way in online learning and establishing extended campuses across the United States and around the world.

The university's noted history and fame also include a haunting well-known to students, faculty, and staff for years.

A Nun's Ghost?

Stories tell of a very young nun who found herself pregnant after a scandalous indiscretion, some say with a priest. Distraught, so the stories go, she threw herself from a fourth-floor window of Loretto Hall, one of the campus dormitories at the time. Other versions of the tale say she was pushed—by the same priest she'd had the affair with. There are no further details offered in the stories, no names or dates to make concrete the rumors of a young nun's disgrace and death. All the proof available are the sightings of a dark, hooded form that many describe as resembling a nun in full habit—a figure, interestingly, that was never reported until after the school's break from the Catholic Church and transition to lay leadership in the 1960s.

For years, the ghost has been witnessed in Loretto Hall and the nearby Webster Hall and Maria Hall by students, faculty, and staff alike. In addition to appearing to the unsuspecting, the ghostly activity has included lights shutting off and turning on for no apparent reason, closet and wardrobe doors opening on their own, and even a student's guitar being strummed—while put away under a bed.

Billy Ratz is the Alumni & Parent Relations Officer in Webster University's Office of Advancement. What's more, he's a Webster graduate who heard the tales of the nunlike apparition from friends who lived in the dorms of Loretto Hall while he was a student. "I never lived in this part of campus," he told me when we met at his office on Loretto Hall's fourth floor, "so I never had any firsthand experiences or anything like that then. But there were always stories—when I was an undergrad—stories of people hearing the ghost or feeling it. Or weird stuff like doors slamming or books randomly falling off of bookshelves—stuff like that. But it was mostly people feeling a presence."

Billy offered me a seat and eased back in his desk chair. Webster University knickknacks crowded his office, peering out from among the family keepsakes and the mementos of his hometown of San Diego, California. In a well-packed bookcase against the wall, I spotted two volumes I was familiar with on St. Louis-area ghost encounters—including Loretto Hall.

"This whole building used to be a dormitory," he explained. "It's all offices currently."

EYEWITNESS

But we weren't there to discuss the history of the university and the changing use of its original buildings through the years. Or even to share tales of others' unexplained experiences on campus. In my research, I'd found Billy's name figuring prominently as I looked into accounts of the ghostly happenings at Webster University because he himself had encountered the spectral nun that haunts Loretto Hall.

Twice.

"The first time I saw her, it was my first Homecoming weekend as a member of this staff," he began. "I was up here with an alumni volunteer. That year's homecoming theme was *The Wizard of Oz*, and the alum had to come back up here to change out of her costume. So she went in the women's restroom and I said I'd wait out by the receptionist's desk."

Coming off the elevator, I'd passed the receptionist's desk as I made my way to Billy's office. Like most reception areas, the one on Loretto Hall's fourth floor faced the elevator, which was separated from the reception area by a long corridor that cut between them as it ran straight from the front of the building all the way to the rear.

"It was evening, maybe eight o'clock or eight-thirty, and it was dark." He gestured at the ceiling. "At night in here, only half the lights are on, every other one. So I was just waiting around and happened to look down the hall. Back then, the back part of the building was still dorms, and there was a big fire door partway down the main hall that separated the office part of the building from the dorm side of the building.

"Right in front of the fire door, I saw this dark, shadowy, hooded figure come out of the file room. It stopped as it crossed the hall, and it felt like it turned and looked at me. Then it turned back, continued across the hall, and vanished into the wall."

Billy shuddered still, as he recalled the encounter. "I instantly had chills. It freaked me out!"

I asked him to describe the figure he saw. Could he make out any details? Did it seem like a person? A shadow?

"It seemed like a person," he began, "I didn't see a face—it was all dark under the hood. It's funny, it was more ... it was little transparent, but dark, just this dark form. I couldn't see through it, really, but it was dark in the building and I was at the other end of the hall." The distance he was describing, I estimated from my walk to his office, was probably fifty or sixty feet. Hard enough to make out detail in the gloom at that range, it was probably even harder with the shock of the sudden and fleeting appearance of the apparition.

Billy continued, "A few minutes later, the alum came out of the restroom and I said, 'We're getting out of here!' I told her what I saw. She knew the stories from when she was a student here and agreed we should get out. So we left.

"Now, the funny thing is, about two weeks later, a co-worker of mine—who has since left—was working late here and saw the *same thing*. The exact same thing! He was standing up by the receptionist's desk in the exact same spot I was. It was around the same time, eight-ish. He was working late, with half the lights out, and he saw her—the ghost! She was closer to him, though, further up the hall when she crossed it. He was dead serious when he told me about it. 'It was really freaky, Billy,' he said to me and I was like, 'I know! Tell me about it!'" Billy laughed.

"That was the first time I saw the ghost.

"About six years later, I was standing at the receptionist's desk—only this time, it was the middle of the day, like around one o'clock in the afternoon. I was talking to our receptionist, with my back to the elevator. I had this sense somebody had just come off the elevator and was coming up behind me to the receptionist's desk. I just kinda glanced quickly backwards, over my shoulder, and I saw that same hooded figure I'd seen before!

"I quickly turned back to the receptionist and she looked at me, eyes wide, and said, 'Billy, are you okay? You're as pale as can be!' She was facing the elevator where I just looked so I asked her, 'Did you see anything?' 'No,' she said. 'Oh my God,' I said, 'the ghost was just right behind me!'"

The daytime apparition intrigued me. I asked Billy if she looked the same in daylight as she did the in the night when he saw her cross the hall.

"It was the same figure, but *right behind me.* She was a lighter gray color—I figure because it was light out, like watching a movie when the lights are on—but still this gray, shrouded figure. I couldn't see her face again.

"Now, the scary thing about this time: about five minutes later, one of my co-workers, who has since retired, was standing at the receptionist's desk in the exact same spot, talking with the receptionist exactly like I was, and all of a sudden the receptionist looked at her, eyes wide, and said, 'Are you okay? You're as pale as can be!' And my co-worker said, 'I felt like there was somebody behind me!' Now, she didn't see anything, but she had the strongest feeling somebody was right behind her, and nobody was there.

"Weirdly, as far as I've heard, the only people who've ever seen the ghost have been men. Women have felt her presence, but they don't see her. Many of my co-workers have worked late and *felt* something on our floor.

"It's freaky. You just don't expect to see something out of the ordinary. But from the stories I've heard, she's never tried to really spook anybody. You know how you hear about ghosts who try to come after someone? She's never been like that."

As we wrapped up our interview, Billy did make one point that surprised me: In spite of the goosebumps and blood-chilling shock of his two run-ins with the Loretto Hall ghost, he's actually eager for a third encounter.

"I look forward to working after hours because I hope I'll see her again. I want to see her closer up. I sometimes walk the hall when I'm alone, looking. I'm not scared of her. I just want to see her again—I never believed in ghosts until I saw her."

Firsthand Accounts

Selma Avenue

"You'll think I'm crazy," the message began, "but I don't talk about this in my house. It makes our, um, *roommates* act up."

I met J—— at small café one afternoon. It was bright and sunny, bordering on hot. Shaking her hand, J—— seemed to me like she could have been one of any of the young moms from my own kids' grade school. "I'm fortunate to live in the house I grew up in," she told me, taking a sip from her coffee. "My house was built around 1907, I think. It's an old neighborhood. Almost all the houses around my house are over a hundred years old. My parents bought the place in 1977. And I was born a few years later.

"When I was little, I used to hear someone calling me from down the steps. I thought I was crazy, and my mom used to always tell me 'Oh, you're hearing things,' but it was always the same voice I heard, and I always knew right where it came from. I never saw anything, but weird things used to happen, like doors closing and things falling off of shelves when nobody was in the room. It never felt scary, just inconvenient."

THE LADY ON THE STEPS

She settled back in her chair. "The house is an old American Foursquare, two stories and four bedrooms, where my mom and I lived through my childhood and teens.

"About a year after my parents divorced, when I was about seven or eight, I was living in the house with my mom, just the two of us. Our bedroom doors were right next to each other, upstairs. I remember waking up one

43

night and I walked out of my bedroom and there was a woman standing there on the steps, just glaring at me. She had on an antique dress, like colonial or maybe civil war, but old looking. I could probably draw her face for you, she was so vivid. She was transparent, but right there, shifting her weight from one foot to the other. I froze. She did *not* look friendly. She looked irritated—with me—and she just stared me right in the eye. She looked past me for a moment, then went back to staring at me. I was frozen and couldn't go anywhere. I remember finally getting up enough energy to call my mom: 'Mom... *Mo-om!*' I don't remember what I said exactly because all could think was how I had to get away from this ghost in my house! It was terrifying!

"My mom finally walked out and looked down the steps and looked at me and said, 'Just come to my room.' I still couldn't move. I was like, 'Uh, mom, there's a ghost right here.' 'It's just a shadow,' she told me, 'you're seeing lights from the neighbor's house. Come in my room.' It was a while before I could eventually pull myself through the hallway—past the steps! The Lady could have come up those steps!—and into my mom's room. I don't remember anything else, so I guess I went back to sleep, and everything was fine. The next morning, I said to my mom, 'There was a ghost on the steps!' and she said, 'You're fine. There was nobody there. I don't know what you're talking about. Your mind was playing tricks on you.'

"Ten years later, I was in high school and she admitted to me she saw it that night, too! She said she looked down the steps and saw the lady and how she was looking at me. My mom didn't want to scare me so she just started telling me everything was fine and to come to her room. I mean, what else are you going to do?

"She later told me she saw the lady two other times after that. And every time it was when I was in trouble. Like, I got in a car accident one night. It was very minor, but I was late by a few hours and the entire time I was gone, my mother was sitting on the couch and she looked up and there's the lady, on the steps, glaring at her, looking really, really angry.

"She's still there now. I haven't seen her like I did before, but even last night, I mentioned to my husband I was coming out to talk to you about this and I saw her, as a shadow on the steps. It was right next to my shadow on the wall. There was nothing there that should have been casting that other shadow.

"She's definitely still there. When she goes up and down the stairs, you can feel that she's there. I don't know how to explain it, but sometimes she's just *there* more than others. My boys have found her a few times. They haven't seen her, but there's this one spot they never want to go past, and it's her spot. I've never told them about it, so they don't know. But that spot on the steps ... they'll tell me it's too scary, that they don't want to go up there, or that they won't walk past it without their father or me. They'll happily go anywhere else in the entire house. But not that one little spot on the steps. She's definitely still there.

"My mom was cool with her. She said she and the Lady just coexisted in the house, so I guess she trusted this apparition after living for decades in the house with her. It didn't bother her! The weird part is, I think the Lady on the Steps looks after me. But I don't know why she gives me that dirty look. She seems *so* mad at me! I try to talk to her. I tell her, 'You can stay here as long as you want, but I just don't want to see you.'

"I don't know any history on our house. If the lady was in some horrific accident on that spot, with that old-fashioned dress, it would have had to have been before our house was there. But she's not alone."

THE LITTLE MAN

"God forbid we should have just one ghost." J——
leaned in and chuckled. "We've got another weird one. We
call this one 'the Little Man'—we give them great names,
don't we? The Little Man only appears to children. And you
don't have to live in the house to see him—you can just
be visiting. This ... this is a super-weird one. I remember
seeing him when I was a child. He was not a full-grown
human. I remember him only being this big," J—— held a
hand about a twelve inches above the table where we sat.
"He was maybe a foot tall, max. Everyone who's seen him
has described him as a different size. This is the weird
part—you think when you're going to see a ghost, you'll
see a person of regular size. When I was little, I described
him as looking like the Schnucks soldier boy.* I looked it
up, and I think the Little Man's gear actually looks more
English than American.

"When I was little, he talked to me. And he was so nice!
He would tell me things like 'Don't yell at your parents'
or 'You shouldn't scream in the house' or 'Be nice to your
mother'. He'd also tell me about his family. He had two
children, a wife ... it was interesting.

"But he had one very strict rule. In my room, there was
a light switch cover on the wall. My mother made it, so
it wasn't old or original to the house or anything. But he
didn't like anyone touching it." J—— laughed nervously.
"I feel insane explaining this. Completely crazy."

I assured her she didn't sound crazy. Like someone
dealing with something wildly out of the ordinary, sure.
But she seemed completely reasonable.

"I used to tell my mom about this and it freaked her
out. Scared her. She could see the Lady on the Steps and
be okay, but she did *not* like me talking about the Little

---

*Schnucks is a Midwest grocery chain that's used a stylized Colonial-era
American soldier as its mascot since the 1960s.*

Man. It always made her uncomfortable. She'd let me go on with it sometimes, but it wasn't her favorite.

"Years later, we'd made that bedroom into a guest room. My mom had a friend whose little boy took a nap in there. He came out later and said 'Where did that little man come from?' My mom did not want to talk about it, even as he told us how a little man came to see him.

"When my brother was little, he used to see the Little Man. But he was scared of him. I don't know why—he never would talk about it. Over the years, my nieces saw the Little Man. And one of my sons has seen him.

"My older son's room has a lot of activity in it, like a closet door that opens and closes by itself, for no reason, all the time. He came to me one night. It was an especially creepy night in his room, and when that happens, we just kinda talk it out. 'Everybody calm down. Everybody take a break... Everybody here is friends.' Such a weird thing to have to say to the empty air in your house, but it seems to work pretty well. So the next morning, my son comes to me and asks, 'When did you guys let me have a hologram in my room?' He told us he woke up again in the middle of the night, and there was a little man in his room.

"When he appeared to my son he was taller, like two or three feet. My son said every time he woke up that night, he saw it walk in and out of his door, a little soldier that looked like the Schnucks soldier boy." That last detail, J—— told me, was particularly eerie because she and her husband don't talk to the kids about the things that have appeared in the house. Her older son has seen the Little Man and has caught a few other things happening, while her younger son has had only one experience. She paused, thoughtful. "My mom passed away a while ago, and my younger son says she comes to see him. He came to me one morning and told me, 'I woke up last night, but then Grammy came to sing be back to sleep.' Weirder things have happened in

47

our house, and my toddler's grandmother coming to sing him to sleep is absolutely fine with me."

THE DARK CORNER OF THE BASEMENT

"We have things falling over in the basement sometimes," J—— continued, "and when it happens I just want to get the hell out of there."

She told me it's not so bad anymore, since her husband set up a workshop in the basement and spends more time down there. "But before that—and actually back when I was a kid—there was one section of the basement that was really dark. I can't explain it more than that or exactly what it was. It just felt terrifying. There are other parts of the house that aren't so well lit, but nothing like that. I'm not afraid to walk into a dark bathroom with the light off, but I would not go in this dark corner of the basement. Our dogs wouldn't go down there. Nobody wanted to go down there. If I had friends over when I was a kid, and we went in the basement for some reason, nobody would want to go back to that corner. Until my husband set up his workshop—that's really changed the energy down there—things would get taken off the shelves. Tools, an old radio ... you'd go down there and find them set on the floor, in front of the shelves."

THE RUNNING SMELL

"We were remodelling," J—— recalled for me, "and on the stairway to the basement, we'd pulled off a bit of the wall and we noticed something behind it. We removed the piece of wood and found this newspaper, just sitting there in the wall. It was from 1906 or 1907, the sports section and a section with cartoons about Teddy Roosevelt. We could never figure out why it was in there. I mean, sometimes in old houses you'll find newspaper wrapped around a pipe as insulation. This was not that. It was just a newspaper page stuck inside the wall. It was kinda cool and we removed it and had it out for maybe a couple weeks.

"In this time, something began running up the stairs from the basement to the attic. And that was when we started noticing this smell that would travel up and down the steps. It was so bizarre. You would stand on the stairs and the Smell would just shoot past you. It was so pungent! It was like sewage, *really* bad! It wasn't like sulfur—apparently, if you smell sulfur, you should run out of the house.* Ours was just a bad sewage smell you could follow up and down the stairs. It would race all the way from the attic to the basement and back up, running frantic. If you stood on the steps, you could smell it two or three times in ten minutes—that's how fast it was going. There were no sounds of footsteps with it, but you could feel it go past you. Sometimes the Smell would follow you into a room for a little bit, but then it would leave again.

"We thought maybe it had to do with the newspaper, and we read all through the sports news and the Teddy Roosevelt cartoons and there was just nothing that made any sense as being connected to what was going on in the house with the Smell. Going over it again and again, we finally found this notice, a little tiny blurb about a man named César who had gone into the woods and had a hunting accident while he was alone. So, we started talking to the Smell and trying to figure out if it was him. We didn't really get any answers and the Smell never stopped. So we put the newspaper back where we found it in the wall and said, 'Well if this was you, we know that you were here.'

"After that the Smell went away." She laughed, shaking her head. "I wish we'd have figured that out sooner. It smelled *really* bad."

According to some paranormal researchers and demonologists, an odor of sulfur indicates a demonic presence.

Dead Spots and Weird, Creepy Stuff

"We hear doors open. Sometimes we just find them open. We hear footsteps on the stairs, but not consistently—it'll go on for like a week, and then just stop. There's certain spots in the house that, when things get more active—doors open and stuff comes off the shelves—the electronics in these places stop working. We have a couple places that have become Wi-Fi dead zones. They worked fine for years, then one day just stopped. And all the electronics in those areas become fried. So far, it's a TV, a receiver, a Wii ... actually, the Wii just started working again... But the TV, we had to hardwire it to get it to work where it is. Even then, its reception is real hit-and-miss. It'll work fine for a while and then suddenly it just doesn't. And around that time, all the doors and cabinets are open again...

"Whenever I was pregnant, things were very active. When I was pregnant with my first son I used to feel something going past me on the steps all the time. And one day, that something stopped and pushed me. I fell down—just one step—and then I got really angry. I yelled at it, and it didn't happen anymore. It was almost like a child, just going crazy tearing up the steps. I really think was a kid. I was pushed pretty low, like in the hip, and I feel like an adult would have pushed me higher, like up in my shoulders. This felt lower, like the size of a five-year-old. Not someone trying to cause trouble, just trying to have a good time ... by pushing people on the steps. Kids don't have any sense.

"I don't know what it is about the steps. I don't know why we have the Lady on the steps, why we have the kid running up and down the steps, why we had the Smell on the steps. Usually, if something happens, it's gonna happen on the steps."

"We've had people who've spent the night in the house end up seriously creeped out. No one's ever mentioned seeing anything, but one person sleeping in the living room heard footsteps walking back and forth between the dining room and the living room. She did not sleep all night. And there was a short period of time when our dogs would run around staring at the ceiling and barking. That went on for a couple years. They'd never do it anywhere else, only at our house.

"There have been times I've been in the shower and something falls on my head out of nowhere. There's a ledge at the top of the shower and we keep things there—shampoo bottle, conditioner, stuff like that. Just out of nowhere one will drop and bounce off my shoulder or head. Things just don't flip themselves off a shelf like that!

"About once a year, in the fall, we'll have cabinets opening and things falling all over the house. Little things like cups and glasses, books, small toys. Fall is the worst, leading up to Halloween. It gets really horrible on Halloween. For some reason, they just love Halloween. It's one of the most active times. That's when, if you're going to have something happen, that's when it's going to happen."

That made sense to me. Tradition holds that the divide between the worlds of the living and the dead grows thinner through the fall, becoming its thinnest on Halloween. Spirits, then, have an easier time reaching across into this world during that season. J—— was unfamiliar with that tradition, but agreed it made sense with her Halloween experiences over the years.

"It's never really scary to me, but I'm pretty much just used to it," she continued. "Though if it starts getting really creepy, another weird thing is that none of the creepiness goes on in the master bedroom. It's like the safe zone. There's some sort of respect about the master bedroom and none of our 'roommates' ever mess around in there."

I stopped J—— there. It occurred to me that in her story about the first night she encountered The Lady on

the Steps, her mother had coaxed her back to *her* room—
the master bedroom. I wondered if maybe her mother
knew it was safe from the activity in the rest of the house.
"Good point," J—— agreed, considering. "Maybe she knew.
I don't know."

CRAZY BUT COMFORTABLE

I watched J—— sit back in her chair and take another
sip of her coffee. There'd been certain anxiousness to her
as she narrated her lifelong experiences in her house, a
tension that had slowly drained as we chatted. "This is
the kind of stuff you can't tell most people because they'll
think you're insane. We get a lot of weird stuff. My older
son and I always know what's going on, hear what's going
on. We're the ones who can talk to them." She laughed once
again. "They're especially aggressive toward me because
they've known me so long. My husband and younger son,
luckily, seem immune. I don't know why it is. My husband
asked me, 'Why do we still live here? This place is nuts!'

"But it's comfortable, "she told me happily, perhaps a
bit resigned. "I've always had the sense the Lady on the
Steps has been looking after me, even though she always
looks so angry. I'd like to have more information, and I'd
love to talk to someone who lived there before us and see
if they've experienced any of these things in the house."

Theatre Lane –
The Theatre Guild
of Webster Groves

At first glance, you might mistake the Theatre Guild of Webster Groves for just another of the large, century-old homes the neighborhoods here are known for. Shaded by the tall trees of Theatre Lane, except for the letter board out front that lists the current production and upcoming shows, the tiny community theatre in the big, white-trimmed, shingle-walled Victorian house blends in perfectly among the single-family homes surrounding it.

Including, like much of Webster Groves, having its share of ghostly residents.

Built in 1909 as *Miss Mulroy's Suburban School of Music*, it was originally a music hall and nursery school and later a printer's shop. For a time it was even a church, the Webster Groves Baptist congregation meeting there while waiting for construction of their church to be completed. Today the building is a designated historical landmark, and home to the longest continuously-running community theatre west of the Mississippi River. The Webster Groves Theatre Guild purchased the building in 1951 and has been staging performances there through the decades since.

FIRST FLOOR: FOOTSTEPS, FACES,
AND THE GIRL ON THE STAIRS

"We hear footsteps," said the guild's official historian, Debbie Love. The first floor is the theatre's lobby, a small entry hall that opens onto a large parlor. The aged hardwood floor creaked under our feet. The wood trim was thick with decades of paint, and the walls of the parlor were adorned with black-and-white cast photos from the past eighty-eight seasons of guild productions—photos in which the theatre's local patrons regularly point out grandparents, great-grandparents, and other family. Standing in the lobby, Debbie indicated the old wooden stairs that wound up to the second floor along the north wall.

"We've had many people who were working down here on props or sewing a costume for one of our plays hear footsteps running up and down the steps or walking across the floor upstairs in the theatre—when they know they're here alone. They get up, and go look at the stairs, and there's no one there. We've also had some of the guys working on the stage, building the sets and so on, hear somebody coming up. One guy was working up there and was expecting another guy to show up and help. He heard someone coming up the steps and called to him, to let him know, 'Hey, I'm up here working on the set!' He waited—the other guy was supposed to have supplies he needed—and waited and finally got up and went to the stairs to look. No one was there."

"One time, we all came early and were sitting here in the parlor going over our lines, three or four of us, quietly. Our director was putting things out for the performance, getting coffee ready. We all could hear somebody walking around upstairs, in high heels—you know how that sounds—and the director comes out and goes 'Who's here?' 'Nobody but us,' the rest of us said. But we'd all heard it, too. She stopped, got a little pale, and said, 'I'm going outside.' That shook her, and even now, she won't go downstairs in the basement here without somebody with her."

"My husband was alone here locking up one night, out on the front steps." She pushed the curtain over the window aside, providing a clear view of the wood-railed porch and the steps leading down to the front walk. "And he turned back to see a lady's face just looking out of the side window, like this..." Debbie leaned her face in front of the window, as if she was checking to see if someone was on the porch. "My husband saw that and was like—" she gave a big, theatrical stage shiver "— and he just took off out of here, real fast!"

She showed me to the front doors of the theatre, a pair of wide, wooden doors, each with a large oval of glass set in the upper half. "Now here—we've had a few investigations of the hauntings here at the theatre. One time, when they were wrapping up and putting their stuff away, one guy turned and took a picture of the doors. And later, when they looked at it—" she ran her fingers over the bottom edge of the right-hand door's window, "—you could see a face just peering over the bottom edge right here."

Debbie then pointed to the first landing on the staircase. "One night when we had the investigators in, we had a video camera here in the lobby pointed up at the stairs. We decided to go up to the theatre. In the video later, you could see the whole bunch of us going up the steps. And just as we got to the bottom of the stairs, you could see, right here on the landing, an angry man! He looked almost like a pirate, with a moustache and a big, black beard and long hair. He was just glaring, really angry looking. It was just his face, no body. Right in front of the wall. And there was a lady's face beside him. They were just looking at us as we were going up."

At each of the back corners of the parlor was a door. These led to the men's and women's dressing rooms. "Back here in the ladies' dressing room, we have a little girl," Debbie explained. "Her name is Ellie—at least that's what one of the psychics that came with the investigators once told us—and she likes to hide in the little-bitty restroom tucked in the back corner here." One side of the room was lined with the lighted mirrors of the dressing stations.

The other side was crowded with costume racks crammed with dresses and coats and accessories for the actresses in that afternoon's upcoming matinee. Right beside the racks was another door. "That door leads to the backstage area upstairs." Debbie opened it to reveal a narrow servant staircase. "One time, when it was really hot, we had this door propped open to get some air through," she recalled. "One of our actresses was sitting here, putting on her makeup and getting ready for the show. She heard a rustle of fabric and in the mirror, she saw behind her, through the open door, the bottom edge of a long, old-fashioned dress—like someone was walking up the steps. It disappeared behind the doorframe, and when she got up and looked, there was no one on the stairs."

SECOND FLOOR: BUD/GUS/CHARLIE, MRS. H IN THE CORNER, AND STOP KICKING MY SEAT!

The old wooden steps groaned, our footfalls plain and distinct on the main staircase as Debbie and I climbed to the guild's second-floor theatre. It's a small auditorium, and with a stage the size of a good-sized living room and seating for less than 150 people, there are no bad seats in the house.

But there are a couple haunted ones.

"We have Mrs. H," Debbie said as she led me to the last row. "She's in the corner, all the way back here." She and I made our way to the very last seat in the row. "We don't really know her name. When the investigators came, they sat in the seat right here, next to the corner seat, with a little temperature gauge gadget." Debbie waved her hand over the corner seat. "They checked the one next to it and in front of it, and when they checked the corner seat, the temperature dropped like ten degrees!" Debbie shivered as she finished. Cold spots—highly localized drops in temperature with no apparent natural explanation for the change like Debbie described—are typically considered by ghost researches to be signs of the presence of a ghost in that space. Finding that cold spot, they believe, means they've located the ghost.

"The funny part is," Debbie continued, "She's not ours. Mrs. H came with the seats." She explained that the theatre seating was acquired from a university theatre in Michigan that was updating and rehabbing. It was only after the guild acquired the seats from the school, she said, that Mrs. H became a presence in the theatre. "She doesn't do anything except watch the plays," Debbie told me. And no one, she said, has ever seen anything unusual in that corner.

We went to the back corner opposite Mrs. H's corner, where the theatre's technical booth was located. "One of our directors was closing up the building after a show and forgot to click off the stage lights." Debbie recounted. "So he trudged all the way back here by the booth—the only way to click off the stage lights is with this switch—and turned everything off. He started down the main aisle toward the stage and the exit when he heard footsteps on the floor behind him, like somebody following him. He stopped, and the footsteps stopped. He started and they started again, and he just ran for it!"

Continuing down to the front of the theatre, Debbie stopped about halfway and pointed out an aisle seat to the right. "Right on the end here, one of our members was at one of our shows, just sitting here enjoying the play, until he felt this kick on the back of his seat. And then another. Someone behind him was just kicking his seat over and over through the whole first act. He decided that at intermission he was going to get the kid who was doing it and let the parents have it. When the lights came up, he stood up and turned around, and the seat behind him was empty. Not only that, the *entire row* was empty. Nobody there! After intermission, he took his seat again, and once the second act got going—" Debbie tapped the back of the seat a few times with her foot. "—it started up again! He looked over his shoulder, and there was still nobody in that whole row. It went on for the rest of the play."

This time, it was my turn to shiver. Only a few weeks before, I'd attended a matinee performance of a friend's comedy group at the guild's theatre, and sat in that very seat. But the weird part? I had a couple of friends sitting in the row in front of me, and when I took my seat, one had looked over her shoulder and joked that I could sit behind her only as long as I didn't kick her seat... "Oh, you were *lucky*," Debbie breathed when I shared my story with her. "Maybe the ghost didn't do anything since you were already talking about kicking seats?"

After turning on the lights from the technical booth, we took to the stage. Again, it's no larger than some living rooms. The set's somewhat consistent show to show, basic, with a backdrop across the back wall and two angled walls stretching from the edge of the stage almost to the back, leaving a gap for the actors to exit and enter from backstage.

"We have a young lady who won't come back here and do shows with us anymore because of the stage ghost, Bud/Gus/Charlie." She led me to the wings to our right. "Bud/Gus/Charlie stays on stage left," she explained. "This actress was in a lot of plays. But when she was waiting right here in the wings for her cue to come out, she'd feel somebody tug on her shirt or tap her on the shoulder and she'd turn and there'd be nobody there. One time, she was waiting and she heard a whispery voice behind her call her name. She came out and just blew the scene—she was so freaked out and couldn't remember her lines."

"Another time, I was the AD* for a play. I had to get here early to get things set up on stage. We had a lot of dishes

Assistant Director

58

for that show, and I would collect them all—all the plates, all the glassware, all the cups—from the stage and take them downstairs to the kitchen to clean them before the show. We had a lady, Diane, in charge of the door, to take tickets and whatnot, and she called up to ask me a question. I was at the top of the stairs with all these dishes and I was about to answer when I hears something behind me, on the stage. I turned around, and right here—" she crossed to stage right and pointed out the gap on that side of the stage between the wings and the crossover area behind the backdrop. "—I saw somebody walk by."

She exhaled, blowing out a long, slow breath before continuing. "It was a guy, with black hair. He had a white shirt on, with the sleeves rolled up, and dark slacks." Debbie's eyes bugged wide. "I didn't even go to look. I turned around and went downstairs with my dishes. 'Is anybody else here?' I asked Diane at the door. Before she could answer, our director stepped out. He was wearing a green shirt buttoned at the wrist and looked nothing like the man I just saw. 'No, just Diane,' he said. 'Well, it ain't Diane that I saw!' I said. The figure I saw looked just like a person walking by, completely solid, no glowing or floating or anything. I went ahead and washed everything and brought it back up. In the theatre, I started calling out, 'I'm here! I'm here! I hope you're not around!'

"We found out later, as we learned about the history of the building, that two brothers used to own this place and they had a printing business they ran up here. I thought, 'That's what the man in the white shirt looked like—an old-time printer.' One of the brothers was supposed to be a prankster, and we think that's who Bud/Gus/Charlie is.

"I call him Bud/Gus/Charlie because we've had three different haunting investigation groups out here through the years, and the psychics that came with each came up with a different name for the ghost up here on stage. One of them got Bud, one of them got Gus, and one of them got Charlie. He's a prankster, so that's probably why they keep getting different names from him. So we just call our ghost Bud/Gus/Charlie.

"When we had our production of *Nunsensations*, all the actresses were getting in line downstage for their big Rockettes-style kickline. I was back there in the lighting booth running the lights that night. I was watching the play to make sure I got all my cues to click on and off all the lights. And the last girl to get in line—now, this was during the show—all of a sudden she stopped, while all the other girls were dancing in their nun habits, and started looking all around behind her. Then she finally got in line with the others and started doing the kick. I was wondering 'What the heck was that?' We kept on with the show, and the person doing music, she was set up at a piano on the side apron here, way down stage right. She'd been playing great all night, but out of nowhere, this one song she just messed up. I mean, nowhere *close* to the music. And again I thought, 'What the heck was that?' After the show, she told me, 'Oh my gosh, Debbie! It felt like someone was standing right over me at the piano the whole time!' and then, she tells me, just as she started that song, the one that went wrong, she heard a whispery voice call her name! 'I couldn't concentrate after that!' she said.

"Hearing that, the actress from the nun kickline came up to us. 'Somebody was pulling on my habit! I thought it was our props person trying to hand me something—but there was nobody there!'

"Bud/Gus/Charlie has played all sorts of tricks on the actresses. He really likes the girls! One of our actresses in a show had just a little bit of time—less than a page—to do a complete costume change. She'd have everything she needed laid out on one of the tables downstairs in the dressing room. So, this one night, she exits her scene, rushes downstairs, changes her dress ... and finds none of her other things. No jewelry, no earrings, no watch, So she comes back upstairs to do her next scene, and her character is supposed to be this very rich lady, and she has nothing, none of her accessories for the part. You could tell she was mad. But at intermission, when she went down to the dressing room, all of her things were on the steps! Laid out carefully, one piece was on one step, then another was a few steps down, then another. All the way to the dressing room. A prank like that, played on one of the girls? It had to be Bud/Gus/Charlie."

Once, she shared with me, during a show's rehearsal, the cast was going over their lines with scripts in hand. The assistant director had left a copy of the script open at the foot of the stage, laying on a speaker. When the cast reached the bottom of the page and everyone turned to the next, the top page of the unattended script flipped right over with them. The entire cast saw it happen and everyone stopped. Some went down and inspected the suddenly lively script, checking for any possible drafts that could have blown the page over. Of course, they didn't find one.

Debbie next took me backstage. Like most theatres, backstage at the guild is dark and crowded, with props and set pieces stored out of sight of the audience but handy for the cast and crew. "One time, when we had the set walls down between shows and the investigators in, you could see a shimmering on the wall here. One of the investigators stood in front of it, watching, then started moving his arms around and going side to side and back and forth. He was trying to see if it was a light from one of the windows and if he could block it with his shadow. But he couldn't. The lights were all off up here, and the windows are all covered. They couldn't do anything to make the shimmering change, and it was there for about twenty minutes. About five of us saw it in that time."

BASEMENT: THE FACE ON THE WALL

The guild's stories aren't limited to the theatre and lobby. Debbie opened the door to the basement and I followed her down the plain, wooden, open stairs to where they disappeared into darkness at the bottom. The air was cool and wet, like most old basements after a storm. Though the floor was concrete, the walls were rough stone, spotted in sharp shadows cast by the bare light bulbs she switched on one by one among the low joists of the floor above. We proceeded through narrow aisles cut through floor-to-ceiling racks of costumes and cluttered shelves of lampshades and dishes and other props. The bony legs of tables, chairs, and stools jutted feet-up throughout.

"On one of the investigations, I had two of the guys from the investigation team ask to go in the basement. We never had any reports of anything happening in the basement, but I said 'Sure, okay. But there's nothing down there except our props. Just be careful.' So they went down in there and all of a sudden I heard these shouts and screams and the two fellas came running right back up. I asked what's wrong and they said, 'There's a head down there!' Now, it's a theatre and I thought it was some prop they saw. 'No—nonono!' they insisted, 'it was a *head!*' So we all went down there, all excited. We were looking and looking and we saw it! There was this head! It was the same one from upstairs, with the long hair and the big beard and moustache. He was on the wall, moving from side to side, first this way then that, from the left to the right and back. It wasn't a floating thing, more like a light shining an image on the wall. So we checked the windows, to make sure it wasn't some trick of the light coming in. But all our basement windows are boarded up tight. There were eight of us down there that saw it, and we just watched until it moved finally, off to the left, and disappeared."

We talked some more about the investigations they'd had at the guild as I followed Debbie back upstairs to the parlor. "So, we've had all sorts of good stuff happen," Debbie summed up. "It's a nice haunted house. All our ghosts are friendly. None have ever done anything more than surprise us. Well, that and a little bit of pranking."

Summit Avenue

M—— was excited to tell me her stories—I saw earlier that day she'd posted on Facebook to all her friends that she was going to be interviewed about her haunted house experiences for an upcoming book. After making introductions, I learned she was a hairdresser, which was no surprise—in those few minutes I could see, like the other hairdressers I knew, she had a certain style of her own, was very personable, and had a hairdresser's gift for gab, gossip, and storytelling.

"My house was just one story, probably an old summer or weekend house for someone from the city." M—— told me. "That's my best guess, from the lake that used to be behind it—filled in long ago—and the old, slatted interior walls we found inside the modern walls when rehabbing. Those were an architectural feature of summer homes back in the day. It was right at ninety years old when I bought it and it had been owned by one family for something like fifty years and then another family for around forty years before that."

It Started with the Kitchen Windows

"I bought the house and moved into it in February, so it was cold out. The first thing that happened, I'd been living there two weeks or so. I was living all by myself—well, I had three cats and a dog at the time. I was asleep, and woke up in the middle of the night and it was freezing cold in the house. I got up to see what was happening, and walking around the first floor, I went in the kitchen and found the windows wide open. They were the kind that latch in the middle and swing in toward you, so it was like walking in and seeing a couple open doors.

"My first inclination was that someone had broken in, that somebody was there. I looked around, didn't see anybody. I was kinda panicking. The purchase of the house was somewhat … acrimonious. The lady of the house didn't want to sell. It was a short sale and she didn't want to deal with it. She didn't move out or pack her things and she had to be forced out at the last minute, with a sheriff on site and all that. She was spooky, kinda like something out of a horror movie—it seemed like every time I turned around, she was right there, practically on top of me." M—— feigned a startled jump and laughed. "It was like that, over and over. So, I was a little nervous when this happened with the windows—I was wondering if she was breaking in to my home!

"But the dog was actually calm—that was a good sign, because if someone was in the house, there'd be running around and barking. Plus, I realized the window screens were intact, so nobody had gotten in—they'd have had to put them back up. I thought that was strange, but maybe it was that the latches weren't shut and the wind came up and blew them open. So I shut the windows and latched them and went back to bed.

"Fifteen minutes later, it was cold again. And the windows were open again.

"At that point I wasn't scared. I was irritated. It was two in the morning and I was done—done dealing with this. I closed them again, pushed the latches as tight as I could, shook them to make sure they were jammed closed, and got back to bed again.

"And fifteen minutes later, they were open again.

"Now, this wasn't one set of windows. It was two sets, side by side next to each other, both wide open. I was tired and I was irritated. I was long past afraid. It was almost three in the morning and I was tired and freezing. I just screamed at the room 'For God's sake, just knock it off! I have to get up in the morning!'

"They didn't open again." M—— laughed. "So whoever heard, got it. I realized then something else was going on. I was honestly relieved to think it was just a ghost, and not the previous owner. I thought, 'Now I don't have to call the police!'

"I was telling a friend of mine about it later and he came over to check the windows, sure it was just something with the latches. 'But why was it just the one time this happened?' I asked him, 'If it's the latches, why didn't the windows keep doing it?' He looked them over and couldn't figure anything out. It happened maybe two more times in the two years I lived there. There was no certain thing going on when the windows would do that. It was just 'Oh, it's those damn windows again!'"

THE FIGURE IN THE HALL

"There were a lot of footsteps when there was nobody else there, and I was pretty sure because I lived by myself. It was everywhere in the house. If I was standing in the living room, I'd hear someone in the dining room and I'd turn around and there was nobody there. Or I'd be in the bedroom and I'd think I heard someone coming from the next room and I'd turn and, of course, there was nobody there.

"About a year after I started living there, my boyfriend moved in with me. I can't tell you the numerous times I was in the living room and I would think I saw him, out of the corner of my eye, walking into our bedroom. I'd ask him something like 'Hey, grab me a sweatshirt while you're in there.'

"And then he'd come out of the kitchen—which is on the other side of the house. It happened a lot. It was just a shape I'd notice go by, and it wasn't him.

I'd see it over one shoulder, and then my boyfriend would emerge from a someplace opposite of where I thought he was.

"The basement stairs were in a weird place, aligned between the bedroom and the sitting room. The doorway was at the far end. It was an awkward spot for the door, and I never understood why it was there. Well, what I found out during a renovation was that the original basement door was over on the other side of the house, at the end of this odd little hallway. Apparently there *were* stairs there that went down to the basement and up to the attic. When one of the previous owners did an addition on the house, they moved the stairs and took away the door, making that little hallway. More often than not, I'd see that figure go down that hallway and just dissipate at the end of the hall, right where the original door used to be. That made so much sense—for the longest time I couldn't figure out why he kept walking into that one wall."

I asked M—— to describe the figure for me. I was curious: did it look like a man or a shadow on the wall? Was it solid or transparent? "It was a shadow," she began, "but it wasn't on the wall. It moved down the center of the hall. It was taller, decisively male—nothing feminine at all about its shape or the way it moved. It just had a male energy to it, too, if that makes sense. I can't even tell you how many times I saw it go down that little hall, always that same way toward that stairwell that was no longer there. Probably dozens of times. It was really weird when the cats were all lined up on front of the fireplace and they'd suddenly all look up at the same spot, then turn their heads together, like they were watching something ... *behind me.* There were times when they'd do that and I would just tell myself 'Don't look that way. Don't look over there!'"

NOT AN ART FAN

"One of the more fascinating things that happened... I had this series of photos that someone had given me that actually came from the Chicago Film Festival. The photographer's name is Skrebneski and he's famous for these nude photos. They're very artistic and very pretty, but they're *definitely* nudes. I had them lined up along the wall, on the floor and leaning with their tops against the wall, face out so I could see them to decide the order to hang them.

"I woke up one morning and walked out and all of them were face-down. I didn't hear them fall, and they were fairly large prints, so I thought I would have heard them. And I realized then that didn't make any sense: They were angled up against the wall, and if they'd just slid flat, they would have all been face up. These were all turned face down, all of them."

She shook her head, "I thought, 'That's strange.' But I figured I sleep heavy and just didn't hear. So I picked them all up and leaned them back against the wall. I had three cats running around there, and I didn't want them stepping all over them, putting a foot through one, whatever.

"So, I walked from the living room through the dining room to the kitchen and poured myself a bowl of cereal and I walked back into the living room." M—— paused, laughing as much from nerves as amusement, "and they were all face-down again, just the way I found them before. It was four minutes later, and they were in the exact same place as when I got up. And I didn't hear them at all, which was *really* creepy. 'Okaayyy.' I told myself, 'I guess someone doesn't want these up here.' So I took them all and put them in a stack and leaned them—facing the wall—in the corner. I wasn't going to play this game. Eventually, I just put them away.

"You question yourself a lot when stuff like this is going on 'Did I do that?' then 'Why would I have done that?' always ending on 'Of course I didn't do that!' I'd go to work and tell people 'The craziest thing just happened...' and they'd say 'I can't believe you sleep that house!' But I never sensed a feeling of malevolence or anger. The only thing close to that was the basement. It got kinda creepy."

SOMETHING RIGHT BEHIND YOU IN THE BASEMENT

"I never saw anything in the basement," M—— told me. "But the dog and the cats utterly refused to go down there.

"My dog would stand at the top of the basement steps and stare at me until I came back upstairs. It was like she didn't want me down there, either. But that's where the laundry was, so I went down there fairly often. And she would just stand at the top of the stairs and give me this intense look like, 'You need to get back up here, *right now.*' She would visibly relax physically when I came back up the stairs.

"But there was this one time, the dog was outside in the yard playing with me and she ran into the basement with me when I went to put something away—I kept all the tools and stuff in the little room at the edge of the basement because it was easier to carry them in and out from there than from the garage. All of a sudden, the dog looked around, realized where she was and *boom!* she bolted.

"She goes in the basement in our house now ... she goes up and down stairs ... it was just *that* basement.

"You know that feeling that somebody's right behind you? And then you turn, and of course, nobody's there? Then the feeling subsides—but not completely. I'd be standing there at the washer and..." M—— shivered. "It was a 'Yikes!' kind of thing, y'know? There were a few times I walked *briskly* back up the stairs! But we never saw anything down there, and there was nothing as overt as what we had going on upstairs."

THE LOCKED DOOR

I watched M——'s eyes go wide with sudden recollection. "Here's one more crazy story. This happened right after I moved in. The door that we used to get in and out of the house—not the front door but the kitchen door—had a handset lock and a deadbolt lock on it. The deadbolt worked fine, but the handset... Nobody had a key for it, and it hadn't been used in so long that I guess nobody living there before us thought about it anymore. The handset wouldn't latch when you pulled it closed but I could lock the door using the key with the deadbolt, so it was okay. In fact, I was waiting for a locksmith to come and fix it.

"So, a guy had just come to give me a bid on doing some work on the house and he left. He didn't say anything and just walked out the door. Well, since the door wouldn't latch, two of the cats got out. My cats are not outside cats, so when I realized it I ran out on the porch and I grabbed one and threw it inside and grabbed for the other one. I pulled the door shut to make sure no one else would get out in the meantime. When I turned around to go back in, wrestling this screeching cat, the door wouldn't open.

"It was locked.

"I was thinking, 'It couldn't have locked—I don't have the key in there.' You had to physically put a key in and turn it to lock that door! So I'm standing there trying to figure out what to do with this cat going nuts in my hand and I remember my neighbor across the street is in construction. 'Maybe he has a tool that could possibly help me get the door open,' I thought. Of course, he had nothing. He offered me a hammer so I could bust out a window." M—— rolled her eyes and sighed. "Then he came over and helped me jiggle on the door handle, pull on it, push on it. It wouldn't budge. It was like it was bolted. We were at it for a good fifteen minutes before I gave up and thanked him.

"So I walked around to the side of my house where there's a sunporch. It had those old aluminum windows, so I was pretty sure I could rig something and get one open. So I got one open and got the screen up and I threw the cat inside. Then I tried to get in.

"The bottom of the window was above my waist so I had to lift myself and pull myself over. So I was laying there because I couldn't quite get through. I was half out of the window, in overalls and red gardening clogs. My feet sticking out, I'm sure I looked like the Wicked Witch of the East with the house that landed on her from *The Wizard of Oz*. I was kicking my legs and, honestly, it probably took ten minutes for me to get through the stupid window.

"Finally, I'm in and I'm livid. And now, from laying on that tiny aluminum ridge in the window for ten minutes, I had this stupid bruise across my stomach that made me look like somebody tried to saw me in half. I walked out of the sunporch into the house, and the cats and dog are looking at me like I've lost my mind. I walk up to the kitchen door, and it's totally unlocked. *Totally unlocked!* It just opened! That door had to have been bolted when I was outside. There were two of us working on it, and it wouldn't budge.

"I think I did a yell into the room, 'I've had enough! Enough! I live here, I'm doing nice things to this house— knock it off!'

"Never had a problem with the door since."

A HAUNTED APARTMENT, TOO:
THE LITTLE GREEN ARMY MEN

But the house on Summit wasn't the only haunted home M—— had in Webster Groves. Before her house, she said, she lived in one of the many apartment complexes tucked in among the businesses that line Big Bend Boulevard and Lockwood Avenue. "I knew I wanted to live in Webster, and I thought living in an apartment there for a while would let me explore the neighborhoods and scope out houses," she explained to me. "The apartment was tiny, teeny tiny. A real one-person place to live.

"I actually thought at first someone was breaking in to my apartment. I've talked about it with clients, and one asked if I was sure I didn't have a stalker. I came home one day, and on the dining table where I usually dropped my purse or whatever else I had in my hands, there was a little green army man. One of those little plastic soldiers you get in a bag. It was just sitting there in the middle of the table.

"I looked at it for a minute and decided maybe the kid of one of the previous tenants lost it in a corner of a closet or something and the cats found it while I was gone and just left it there. So I took it and threw it in a drawer.

"And about three months later, I came home, and there was another one.

"It was a different one, too. I lived in that apartment for not quite three years, before I moved to the house on Summit, and I think I collected eight of those little army men. They would just show up. They were always in that same spot, right where I'd see them when I first walked in the door. And they were all different. You know how one little army man has a rifle, another a pistol, another binoculars, and so on? I got like one of each. It was surreal. I have no idea what that is or what it means. I worried someone might be breaking in, but the place had one door and one window, and the window was a sheer thirty foot drop. The door was always secure, the window was always secure. They never looked tampered with, and it felt silly to call the police over some little green army men. It's absurd!"

I noticed the smile had been slowly fading from M——'s face as she told me about the apartment. This wasn't fun for her, like her strange Summit Avenue tales ... in spite of having toys. "The last thing I ever found there... I had a necklace with a little-bitty charm on it that I'd lost probably fifteen years before. I'd lived in at least five different places between the place where I lost it and that apartment.

"I came home one day, and that necklace with the charm was sitting there on the table. In the same spot where the soldiers always were. I cannot even wrap my head around that one. I've never figured it out, and it's never happened again."

Bompart Avenue

I knew that H——'s story would be a bit different from the stories of other homeowners I'd interviewed. Although one or two I'd spoken with had been able to put a name to their haunting, H—— came prepared with an armload of historical documents regarding both his home and the spirit dwelling in it—including a photo of the man from before he passed away.

We sat down for breakfast in a busy Webster Groves café. After we shook hands and gave the waitress our orders, I had to assure H—— that my digital recorder was up to the challenge of registering our conversation over the clinking of flatware and dishes and the natter and grommish of the other restaurant patrons. A pleasant gentleman about the same age as one of my uncles, he was just back from his morning workout. He chatted with me for some time, and we compared our experiences from years of corporate consulting before coming around to his home and the less-explainable occurrences he and his family have encountered there.

A LITTLE BACKGROUND

"It's a Queen Anne style house," H—— began. "It's one of three houses that are all related to each other through Colonel Alexander Hequembourg.

"He bought the land the houses are sitting on with his muster-out pay from the Union Army. The house was built in 1901. Three years later, he built a smaller version of the same house next door, for his daughter. In between the two of them, there's a little bungalow. That bungalow, it turns out, was the workers' cabin for when the construction people came out from the city to work on the houses. They'd spend the week in the workers' cabin and then go back to the city on Friday afternoon. In 1914, that workers' cabin was moved up and made into a house on a foundation in its present location. The woman who lived in that house in 1914 still lived in that house when we moved in to our house in 1984.

"Much to my wife's dismay, I'm an only-child son of an only-child son, and I'm the sole inheritor of all the history of my family. I have trunkloads of correspondence that date back to just post-Revolutionary War. Letters tracking people down—where was Cousin Harry and so on—so I know a lot about where people were and who they were.

"My family has a history of service in the Civil War: My great-grandmother's brother served In the Fifteenth Illinois Volunteers. The gentleman I'm referring to is Lucius W. Barber, and I happen to have an artifact of his from his war time: I have his bayonet. Not a collector's item at all—there's a billion Civil War bayonets around. It's in its scabbard, but as far a Civil War memorabilia goes, it's not uncommon. It's the kind of thing you could pick up at any flea market for twenty bucks."

ENTER THE COLONEL

"I guess I was first introduced to—but not actually made aware of—the Colonel the week we moved into the house.

"We moved into our house from two homes—the apartment that I had and the house my wife had—in *one* weekend—*Banzai!* We had friends helping and boxes and a rental truck and *multiple* trips. By Sunday night, we were all sitting in the middle of the boxes going, "'Oh, shit—we bought a house!'

"So, as we started to uncrate, put things away and into closets, I was working back in an eaves closet. And there, laying against the stud, was my uncle's bayonet. I yelled down the stairs to my wife, 'Did you put my uncle's bayonet up here?' 'No,' she called back, 'I think it's still in the box.' So I went to look in the box, and the bayonet was in the box.

"The bayonet I found belonged to the Colonel."

Now, as unusual as I'm sure it is to just stumble across a Civil War bayonet in an empty house you've just moved into, as H—— himself said, they're fairly common pieces. So I had to ask how he was so sure it was the Colonel's bayonet.

"He was the only other guy to ever own the house," H—— declared with confidence. "We were only the second family ever to title that house. This whole area was out in the boonies back then. And understand, when he bought the land, there was no Webster Groves yet. He bought land in the Town of Fairview, which never materialized. Then it became Tuxedo Junction, which later got annexed to Webster Groves. I'm not sure the Colonel ever actually lived in Webster Groves—when he died, the reports talk about him living in Tuxedo Junction.

"So the only assumption I can make is that the bayonet is the Colonel's. I remember making a joke that he should be friendly because we brought in a bayonet that belonged to a comrade-in-arms who fought on the same side as he during the war—both men were Union officers. I do remember making the comment that at least we shouldn't have any problems, since we're all on the same side."

GAS AND ELECTRIC

"While we were still moving that week, a series of very interesting occurrences happened. And they kept happening until I was forced to admit that this was outside the realm of probability—statistically, this wouldn't happen without some outside influence.

"In a period of three or four days, the trunk lights in both my automobile and my wife's were left on until the batteries drained. Neither of us, in our entire lives, has ever used a trunk light. Never turned it on, never turned it off, never thought about it, *never* used it."

I nodded along, unable to recall ever using the trunk light in any car I've ever owned, except when it would come on automatically when the trunk was opened—and shut off automatically when it was shut.

"In both cars, they were switched on and left on while the trunk was closed.

"So, one evening we were in the house. A lamp on one side of the living room flickered off. My wife got up and walked across the room to play with the switch. Just before she got to the lamp, it turned back on. That happened to me, my wife, and at least one of my daughters—all with different lamps, in different places."

So, it wasn't one faulty lamp, or a poorly wired outlet.

"No, no," H—— laughed. "It would make you get out of your chair and go all the way cross the room before flickering back on.

"Most of the activity revolved around electricity. The Colonel built this house to be lit with gas mantles—the entire house is piped for the gas mantles. In fact, a fantasy I have is that I'd like to get them cleaned up and sealed and do some gas lighting in the house again. If I had to hypothesize, I'd say it's because the Colonel never liked electricity. He considered it dangerous and had a patent distrust of electricity. It was new. He had no fear of gas whatsoever. He understood it. It was how he did things.

"There was another time... In our first year in the house, my wife and I left for a trip to Jamaica and we left a babysitter with the kids. She was a young lady, seventeen or eighteen, and we'd worked out an arrangement with her parents to have her stay with our kids.

"By this time, we'd figured out this electricity thing and we'd all just laugh when a light would go off and blame it on the Colonel. So, this babysitter was playing videos for the kids, and the VCR quit."

His daughter, T——, remembered the incident well. After H—— put us in touch, she related it to me. "I was in maybe in fourth grade and my sister was in second grade. We were in the den downstairs, watching a movie on the VCR when the VCR and the TV just turned off. The babysitter got up to walk across the floor to hit it or do whatever you do to get electronics started again. She got about halfway there and it came back on—by itself. She sat back down and it happened again. She got up again and it came back on again. This repeated maybe four or five times.

"She was definitely getting really scared, and my sister and I weren't bothered at all. We just giggled and said, 'Oh, it's just the Colonel!'

"After our parents came back, we never saw that babysitter again."

IN THE COLONEL'S FOOTSTEPS

H—— explained, "The girls both lived in the house fifteen years or so. They chose not to have any fear about it because the Colonel was a well-meaning guy, and we were living in *his* house. We *got* that, but it was also a case of 'Sorry, guy, there's nothing else to do. You have no relatives left.'

"I don't believe I ever heard it," H—— continued, "but the girls did report from time to time over the years that they thought they heard him walking around upstairs."

T—— did remember the footsteps. "I thought I heard them up and down the hall when I was little, just right outside the bedroom, at night," she told me. Interestingly, though, she didn't agree completely with

H——'s assessment about choosing not to have any fear in the house. The electrical incidents and the footsteps in the hall weren't too troubling to her as a child. But the upstairs sewing room was different.

"I never liked staying in there," she explained haltingly. "And I was always having to stay in there when my grandparents visited and stayed in my room. I didn't like it in there. It was just ... *creepy*. It wasn't dark or anything. It had windows and there were actually little French doors that led to a little widow's walk outside—it was a nice, bright little room. But it was always kinda cold, and it creeped me out and I never liked going in there."

She also pointed out to me that it seemed to her that the activity was more lively in their early years in the house versus their later years. "It was like we were being tested," she offered, pointing out that their family were the first to own the place who weren't descendants of the Colonel.

H—— saw the Colonel's possible objections similarly. "We started asking ourselves, 'Why would he have an issue?' Well, first, we weren't family, and we bought his house—which he had no control over. It was his granddaughter-in-law who sold it to us. His grandson had been hospitalized for several years with Alzheimer's. When she accepted our offer on the place, she looked at the two of us and said, 'You're going to love this house.' And we have. It's felt receptive and warm and loving from the moment we walked into it.

"And here's an interesting coincidence: The next Sunday after we bought the place, we went to services at our church and realized the woman we had just bought a house from was sitting right next to us. She was a founding member of the church we attended, and actually a lot of the foundations of that church were established in our own living room."

THE SENIOR OFFICER'S APPROVAL

"Fast forward, and the girls are grown up and go off to college. Because we'd been funding education for so long, we've done little with the house."

The *kids versus home updates* dilemma I understood all too well. H—— went on to describe the old woodwork and all the effort they put into stripping the aged and damaged lacquer from the wood and refinishing it, everything from the baseboards to the handrail on the stairs. "I think you'll find we're one of the last remaining houses in all of Webster with natural woodwork," he told me proudly. "Everybody else paints it, since it's easier to keep up."

"About three years ago we put a sizable addition on the back of the house. We stipulated to the builder that, for everything we could in the new part, we wanted to look *exactly* like everything in the old part. So I have extremely high-tech windows, but the trim on them is cut with the same knives as cut the trim for the windows in the old part of the house. The baseboard is identical. The picture rail is identical. Everything inside and out looks exactly like the old house. We went to great pains to make sure that everything in the new part paid homage to the old part, so the new and old talked to each other as buildings."

He explained to me why this was important. "An earlier project I did was to replace a ceiling light in the hallway with a chandelier that I had purchased. So, I was up on a ladder—I'm a handyman and have some construction experience—and pulled the old fixture out. The new light wasn't heavy, and I was using the same box in the ceiling to mount it. I got down off the ladder and took one step away … and behind me the new chandelier fell from the ceiling. It stopped, hanging from its wires," H—— held his hands a little under twelve inches apart, "It came this far from breaking into a thousand pieces on the floor.

"Dumb me, I didn't get it. So I get pissed off and go grumbling back up the ladder and put the chandelier back in place, making sure everything's tight. I get down off the ladder and I get two steps away this time and it does *exactly the same thing.*

"And then I got it: The Colonel didn't like what I was doing. I was cutting corners. Using the existing box in the ceiling with the new chandelier wasn't safe. So I stopped, ran down to the hardware store, and got the additional parts I needed. It took me about four hours more to put everything in place. And it stayed.

"Now, if I look at it, in my experiences, what I started doing was fine. It was good enough. But the Colonel ... he wanted it *right.* I understood that the situation was not going to let me leave it that way. But I was taking a shortcut that wasn't the safest way to do it. So no matter how many times I put it up, it was going to do the same thing. And eventually, the answer was going to be the chandelier shattering into a thousand pieces. He was trying to get my attention.

"There are other examples like this and in fact, I suspect, a lot more than I can think of. But after all these years, they're so unspecial that I simply don't record them anymore."

The Colonel's File

H—— reached into the mound of papers he'd brought with him and produced a framed photo that he laid on top of the stack.

"Here," he said.

It was a photo of his house. Black and white, it had that odd mix of depth and flatness that only very old photographs have. It showed his house, without all the houses that surround it now. H—— pointed to a figure seated on the porch, face and shoulders just visible above the porch rail. "There's the Old Man," he said. I gazed at his distant, graying features and wondered what it was like to have uncovered and learned so much about the man whose spirit still inhabited your house.

"My association with these episodes has made me a student of this guy. I know him pretty well." H——'s finger traced over a bay window to one side. "You'll notice the window is missing."

I had. It was odd-looking. The space where the center window of the usual three would be expected was sided over in wood, like the all the exterior walls of the house.

"Now, what was behind there was a huge, eight-foot-tall mirror that came from the old country. In that wall, still, is a cast-iron hook to hang that mirror. When the family moved out, they took it with them. I'd love to get it back. So, this past spring, I decided I'd try to track it down ... and I found the family member who had it died in January."

I was about to commiserate with H—— but noticed then his smile and the twinkle in his eye. "For me, that's just part of the game," he told me. I could see the Colonel and his story had become a fascination for him, and the hunt to uncover his story through papers and personal possessions had grown into a passion.

Most people I interview know nothing of the history of their house, and focus their stories on the unusual experiences they've had in the home. H—— was the reverse: accepting the unusual experiences to the point they they'd become commonplace and forgettable, he had connected with the spirit though the history of the Hequembourg home and family.

"I find the study of the details of ancestors' lives more interesting than the fact their spirit may be around intersecting with us.

"For example, I know the Colonel did gold leafing for a living in his shop downtown—the house out here was a summer place, a country getaway. His brother was a silversmith, and a number of his pieces can be found in the Missouri History Museum." He showed me another photo, this one of a worn, old plaque with the name *Hequembourg* engraved elegantly across it. "This silver plate has never come off my door. I'm sure it was made by the brother."

H—— told me the house was also "inscribed" by the Colonel's grandson. "At least three windows in the house have initials scratched on them. The Colonel's grandson had a diamond ring when he was a kid, and he took it upon himself to scratch his initials in the glass. Also, when we peeled back the wallpaper in my younger daughter's room to re-paper it, on the horsehair plaster below, written in pencil, are two exclamations: one is a declaration of love for a young woman who was not the one he'd eventually marry, and the other says simply, 'The War ended today! — 1917' It doesn't say 'World War I' because there was no World War I back then—it was just *the War*. We re-papered over it, but we know where it is. We think we're going to re-paper in there soon, and this time leave that area exposed and frame it, put it under Plexiglas or something but show that part of the wall with its history."

He sat back, glancing into his mug of morning decaf before taking a sip. "I know more about the family and care less about the ghost."

"I TALK ABOUT THE COLONEL JOYFULLY"

The research H—— had accumulated, and his knowledge of the previous residents of his home and their lives, were impressive. Still, I was curious why he was so sure their unseen housemate with a disdain for all things electrical was Colonel Hequembourg.

"Given we're only the second family to ever title the home, the number of people who it could be hanging around the house is limited." H—— shrugged. "Only

Hequembourgs and Smiths (the Colonel's daughter's married name) were there before us.

"It was a process of putting things together. The bayonet led me to the possibility. That bayonet had been there for fifty years, and the family cleaned that house out when they moved. Why did we find it the day we moved in? Statistically, there's something at play there. I acknowledged it, and offered up as a peace offering my great-great-uncle's bayonet, to let whoever was out there know, 'Hey, we're on the same side.' I must admit, I was doing that comically, but when things started to occur, I grew to accept the idea that this was here, and that we lived with it ... and that he really had our best interests at heart.

"One thing I think that leaves the Colonel comfortable with our family is that we moved in with two little girls, and that's what he had: two little girls. So he *gets* that. It's kind of a 'This is really close to my situation. I have no control over it, but if I could will it, this is how I would will it.'

"I have no problems in a belief that something of this gentlemen is left over and with us. Why must we assume spirits in the house with us mean us ill? There's no need to arrive at that conclusion, other than Hollywood wants us to—it's difficult to make a movie about people who get along with the spirits. Can't sell that!

"People have a tendency to habitually develop fear over these spirits. That was never, ever, *ever* in our relationship with this guy. I like to say that I talk about the Colonel joyfully."

Glennon Drive –
Kenrick Glennon Seminary

When E—— reached out to me, he wasn't sure if I'd be interested in his story. "It happened in Shrewsbury," he said, "and I know you're looking for Webster stories. But it's still 63119.*"

I'm not one to ever pass on a good story, so I informed him it was close enough.

My meeting with E—— was very spur-of-the-moment; he had a busy travel schedule and we'd been unable to find a mutually workable time to sit down. He literally texted me while doing errands one Saturday morning to see if I was free, and fortunately, I had just finished some yard work and was able to get cleaned up in a few minutes to go and sit down with him. When we met, I bought him a green tea and settled in to hear his tale.

"I come from a family of six kids, very religious, very spiritual," E—— began. "Five of us, all the boys, went to seminary. We started at Cardinal Glennon College, which is where I had my experience."

The building opened in 1931 as the St. Louis Preparatory Seminary, offering a program that covered the last two years of high school and four years of college. After years of evolving and developing its programs, in 1987, Kenrick Seminary relocated from its old location to the Glennon Drive campus, forming what is today Kenrick-Glennon Seminary.

"I was there 1974 to 1978." E—— told me. "It was pretty rigid, pretty structured, but we used to hear stories of how

*The zip code for Webster Groves and some of the immediately surrounding areas

85

rigid it used to be, y'know, 'back in the old days.' We were much more relaxed than before, they would tell us. With our schedule, we had breakfast, morning prayers, and classes throughout the day. We'd go off and do stuff, then have dinner, do homework ... and then, about ten o'clock at night, we'd have evening prayers. We'd all go to church, and it took ten or fifteen minutes usually. Afterwards, most everybody went back up to their rooms.

"I have a high metabolism and I always found a way to sneak into the cafeteria," E—— laughed. "They had an ice cream cooler there... Was I supposed to be there? Absolutely not. But I'd always go in there and grab an ice cream out of that cooler—a Nutty-Buddy or an ice cream sandwich or whatever."

He was shaking his head, still unsure about it after all the years. "What happened to me easily happened a dozen times. Now, I always had to be alert when I was down there because the faculty might walk in."

Sure, you *have* to keep an eye out when you're sneaking around...

"I think that only happened once or twice." E—— grinned. "The cooler was up against a wall, so standing at it, the whole cafeteria was behind you—the space where people would eat and the one doorway that led to the hall, where you could get to the faculty area and the student area upstairs or even to the basement space.

"What I started noticing was that, I would look up, and I would see just the last part of a step as someone went by. Like just the last one-fourth of their stride before the doorway blocked my view. What I saw was the exact same thing, time after time. I never saw the face." He held a hand straight up behind his ear. "Only from just about here back, *every time*. They never stopped but always kept walking. It was only that last part I saw—that exact last part of the step—over and over. Just somebody finishing the step. Somebody in a long, black cassock. It was always quiet. There was never a sound that I heard. I would just kinda glance up and catch that last past part of the step.

"At that doorway, you have really three options: one is to go upstairs—that's where we all lived. Two, stay on the same floor—the cafeteria floor—and go to the faculty lounge. There were these glass doors that led to the faculty lounge, they were noisy and squeaky and loud as can be, but I never heard a sound. Three, there was the basement— there was a small TV down there, but it was dark and dingy and only one or two people would ever go down there.

"So I just kept seeing this over and over, night after night, and finally I decided that next time I saw this thing, I'd go running after it and see what I found.

"And the next time I saw it I ran out there. And there was nothing. I ran downstairs, upstairs—I didn't see anybody. And what I realized then was that, at that time, *nobody on campus wore a cassock.*

"I started thinking back and said to myself, my God, there's forty or fifty of us at any given time at night prayers, and whenever I looked around, there was never anybody in a cassock!

"I maybe told one other guy about it, but I never really mentioned it or heard anything like it from anybody else."

I'd looked into it a bit, and by our interview, I'd found nothing about the school related to ghosts or hauntings.

"I've thought about it over the years," E—— said. "I was never scared of it, but I just know that it's something I don't know how to explain."

Turf Court

"I've had a lot of experiences in other places." N——
seemed to apologize, "but our story here isn't super
extensive."

A story's a story, I assured her, and every story helps
fill in the picture of the activity here in Webster Groves.
Besides, her emails had intrigued me when she mentioned
her eight year old daughter had had an experience in the
house as well—and that she wanted to tell me about it. A
few adults had told me of experiences they'd had as children,
but their stories were as seen through the lens of adulthood.
I hadn't yet heard any children's experiences from a child's
point of view and, I must admit, I wondered what a kid
would make of strange goings-on like I'd been told of so
far. N——'s daughter and son sat beside us in the café, a
Kindle and a jumble of little toys scattered over the small
table between them.

BUMPING INTO SOMEONE ON THE WAY TO THE BATHROOM
N—— described her house on Turf Court as a 1950s
bungalow. She thought it was built around 1951, in the
midst of all the post-WWII home building. They'd been
renting the house for three years, she said.

"When we first moved in, I felt like there was an energy
in the hallway." Borrowing my pen, she sketched a quick
layout of the house, showing a long hallway running
along one wall of the living room, separating it from the
bathroom and bedrooms lining the opposite side.

"We had only been there a handful of days. I came out
of the bathroom, walking back into the living room, and ...
it was as if I was going to run into somebody. It felt like

somebody was about to walk into me, and I jumped back to avoid running into them.

"There's been more than one instance since then that I've walked out of the bathroom and almost run into that person. There have been times you could see someone in the hallway. The figures seem very solid when you feel like you're about to run into them. When you see them out of the corner of your eye, they seem less solid.

"Not too long after we moved in V—— was in the bathroom, using the bathroom..." She turned to her young daughter, V——, seated beside her.

V—— spoke up, "Something peeked in."

Something?

"It was a green head," she described. "All green. No hair, no eyes, no ears, no mouth. Just a big, bald, green head with no face. I saw one of his hands—it was green, too—holding the doorframe like people do when they lean in.

"I just kept staring at it. Then, once I went to wash my hands and looked back, it was just gone."

"Mine was *really* creepy," her brother O—— jumped in.

"I should preface some of this," N—— told me, taking a mental step back. "We don't talk about this in the house, so this story is completely unsolicited. O—— just told me today about his experience in the bathroom."

O—— was bouncing in his seat, excited to start his tale. He turned to me. "So, I was taking my shower. I went to grab my washcloth and turned my head to see this guy standing there in the shower with me. He literally looked like another person there! He was in this, like, tuxedo. His tie wasn't tied. It was just around his neck, loose, like he didn't finish tying it."

That gave me pause. The untied necktie was an odd detail for a little kid to add, and it made me consider more carefully O——'s account.

"His face was just blank," O—— continued, "like the face V—— saw. And white. It looked like it had just walked through the wall into the shower. He just stood there. He had this grayish outline around him, like smoke—but it wasn't smoke, which was weird. I blinked, and it was still there, so I was like 'Maybe I'm not imagining things.' And when I reached around again for my washcloth, he just disappeared."

I thanked the kids for their stories and N—— resumed with her experiences in the hall. "Mine was very clearly a person," she said, "*with* facial features. There was no haze, no snow. He had gray hair—" she nodded toward me, "—probably about your age."

That would be an athletic and virile late-forties, for the record.

"He was definitely taller than me," she continued, "maybe five-nine or five-ten.

"Even when there's no figure, you can hear someone walking on the carpet—there's a definite creak in the floor in the hall, so you can always hear when someone's passing through.

"The bathroom door closes by itself sometimes. O—— just told me today he's heard the door to the bathroom shut when he's in the shower and left it open. And none of us are around."

Everything the family had told me so far had centered on that bathroom and the area of the hall immediately in front of it. I wondered if there was activity elsewhere in the house, or any pattern to it in terms of the time of year.

"Everything's concentrated in that bathroom-hallway area." N—— told me. As to when it happens, she considered for a moment and said, "I think it goes in spurts. Sometimes, it will be several times in a week; sometimes months will go by before it happens again. There was a lot of activity when we first moved in, which was in the fall ... you know, thinking about it, we have the most activity in the fall and winter. But maybe that's just because we're home more when it's cold.

"That's about it for we've experienced."

"What about S——?" O—— interrupted.

N——'s eyes sprang wide. "Thank you for reminding me!" she said to her son.

She turned back to me: "Oh, yes. My friend S—— was visiting us, and she was in the living room by herself—I was in the kitchen doing something—and she said, 'Do you hear that?' 'Do I hear what?' I asked. 'I hear piano playing!' And then when I walked in the room with her, it stopped. I did not hear it, but that was when she asked me 'What *was* that?' And I said 'I don't know. I've never heard piano-playing in here before. But that doesn't mean it didn't happen.' And then I proceeded to tell her about some of our other experiences in the house and she got terrified and ran out the door."

O—— was shaking his head. N—— clarified. "Not *literally*," she conceded with a roll of her eyes. "But she's not one who's ever been in that sort of experience before, so she's not real comfortable with it. There was something else that happened when she was visiting, too... S—— was in the living room and heard footsteps in the hall. She knew where we all were and thought it was just the dog trotting through. But then she heard the bathroom door shut and latch, and she knew whatever just went in there, it wasn't the dog."

It's Nothing New

I had to ask: after three years of bumping into fleeting figures on the way to the bathroom and meeting faceless phantoms in the bathroom, what keeps them in the house? Plenty of people would have left after the first shower shared with an apparition.

"This is something I've had experience with since I was a kid," N—— explained. "When I was very, very little, maybe four years old, I had an imaginary friend I played with at my grandmother's house, in the basement. I used to tell my parents about my friend downstairs, who would kind of sit back and watch when I played with the toys down there. He never talked with me, never interacted with me besides sitting there and watching me play, sometimes walking around and having me show him stuff I was playing with.

"So one day, my parents were looking at old photos and I saw a picture of my friend! I pointed it out to them and told them that it was a picture of my friend. That's when I found out it was a picture of my grandfather, who'd passed away years before—in that basement."

She told me of further experiences she had as a teen in her parents' house, including random objects like hairbrushes and bath towels disappearing and relocating on their own, as well as mysterious figures on the stairs and sudden weight sitting on the edge of her bed.

But coming back to why she and her family remain in the house, N—— explained, "I've been in experiences where I've felt threatened, and I've never felt threatened in this house. I think it's just someone who's stuck. For some reason, this guy just wants to hang out.

"We're all just there, and I'm okay with that."

Newport Avenue

"We have stories from our old house," L—— told me when she learned I was looking for tales of ghosts and hauntings in the neighborhood. At L——'s suggestion, we met one Sunday morning. Looking out over her lawn from the shade of her front porch, the grass looked thick and green under a mild sun. We sat there in her porch chairs and chatted for a bit, catching up. L——'s family and mine belonged the same church, and we knew each other from our kids attending the same Webster Groves schools as well.

WE'RE GOING TO NEED A BIGGER HOUSE

"I didn't used to believe in ghosts. Now I do." As L—— began her story, her husband R—— joined us, leaning on the porch rail, hands cradling a mug with his morning coffee. L—— glanced at him. "It was the first house we bought together," she explained, R—— nodding along. "It was on Newport, a little Cape Cod-style bungalow. We bought it as kind of a flip and we'd been there—" she shrugged and looked to R—— "—maybe a year and a half?"

He nodded. "We did a total renovation while we were there. Then we were thinking we needed a bigger house."

"Right," she said, "we were thinking about having a family, so it was time to start getting that house ready to put on the market. As soon as we started doing that, odd things started happening."

That struck me as unusual. Typically, it's the renovations and the rehabbing work to a house that homeowners report rouses the less corporeal residents and stirs up ghostly activity. I stopped them there and asked if they'd experienced anything during the renovation.

"Nothing weird had ever happened at all before we put it on the market," R—— assured me. "We'd been rehabbing the whole time we were there. But things didn't start until we put it up for sale."

L—— picked up again. "We had two Weimaraners at the time. Big dogs. When they wanted to go out in the yard, they'd push on the screen door to make it bang and let us know. It was one of those old wood breeze doors with the spring that pulls it to make it slam shut after you open it. So one night, we were in the kitchen and we hear the slam of the door. So I called out, 'Just a second,' to the dogs and started to get up—and I saw they were sitting on the floor right next to us."

"There's no way that door could open and close on its own," R—— added. "Not in a good wind or anything. So we thought that was kind of weird. About a week later, about six o'clock in the morning... I used to have these remote control cars. I used to run them all over the house, up and down the steps. That morning I woke up hearing the car going." R—— imitated the whine of a toy electric motor, a familiar sound to any parent after a certain number of Christmas mornings. "So I got up and looked around. I looked down the stairs and saw the car going back and forth on the big grate covering the air return in the floor. I figured one of the dogs had gotten the remote and was laying on it. So I went down there and I couldn't find the remote. It turned out it was upstairs in our room—so the car was going by itself. I went to pick it up to shut it off and turned it over to see the switch was *already off*. That was an oddity, but I let it go. From that day on, the dog always sat there and barked at that grate, all the time."

L—— was shaking her head. "That was crazy."

"Now, speaking of crazy," R—— said, "Talk about the one day you were at the window."

A GLIMPSE OUT THE WINDOW

"Okay," she started slowly, "So, I was cleaning the front windows because we were getting ready to have an open house. And I was there wiping, cleaning, cleaning, cleaning, and I caught sight of this woman standing on our front steps. She had short-cropped dark hair," L—— held a hand up along her jaw, right below her ear, "right about to here. And she was wearing this long, white dress. A long, flowing white dress. I turned to get a better look at her, and she was gone. Chills came down my spine and everything.

"R—— was gone that morning, and I saw our neighbor from the house next door outside. We were pretty good friends. Not close, but we'd chat in the yard, garden together, y'know. So, I went up to her and said, 'You're never going to guess what just happened: I was cleaning the window...' and I told her about the woman on my porch disappearing. I described her, the short dark hair and the flowing white dress.

"My neighbor said, 'Why don't you come inside with me for a minute?'"

Never a good sign when hoping for an ordinary explanation in these sorts of stories...

L—— and R—— explained that these neighbors had lived in the house next door for years, and that they had been very close friends with the previous owners of L—— and R——'s home for a long, long time. "So I went in with her." L—— continued, "and she got out a photo album. We were flipping through it and she turned this one page and there was the woman I saw! 'Wait a second...' I said.

"She told me that this woman—the woman in the picture— was her best friend and lived right next door. And that she died in the house next door. *Our house.*

"The picture she was showing me was the woman on her wedding day. I recognized her short-cropped hair and the flowing white dress, which was her wedding dress. I could see my neighbor and her husband in the pictures with her. My neighbor told me that after the woman from the pictures died, her widowed husband just kind of shut down. He sold all of his dead wife's things in a garage sale shortly after, including her wedding dress—the dress I saw her in. Then he sold the house to us right after that. He just wanted out and didn't want to take any of the memories with him, I guess.

"Now, we'd known for a long time that our neighbors had a daughter named L——, same as my name. What my neighbor told me then was that the couple whose house we'd bought had a son named R——," she pointed back at her husband. "Just like him. These two kids with our names grew up together, and were best friends.

"So I started telling my neighbor everything that had been happening, the doors opening and the R/C cars going and the dogs barking. My neighbor put it all together and crafted this theory: that the lady who died in the house didn't want us to go," L——'s voice was trembling at this point. "She pointed out there was this connection with the names L—— and R—— and this love of the house and maybe soon starting a family... She thought her friend's spirit was disgruntled that we were leaving.

"So I went back home and closed the door. R—— was back by then and I told him, 'Get that sign in the front yard—we're outta here!'" They both laughed, remembering.

"I think it was just the set of circumstances," R—— reflected. "The woman passing, the husband leaving so fast, our names matching the kids', and the sale... I think the spirit got caught up in it all."

"It was weird. And when we bought this place," L—— rapped on the porch rail, "we were wondering what we'd find happening here. But so far, after twenty years, it's all been good."

Manchester Road –
The Book House

I wasn't surprised to learn the Book House on Manchester Road was haunted; I was surprised that I'd never before *heard* it was haunted.

Though just to the north and west of Webster Groves proper, the Book House shared the Webster Groves zip code, was within the Webster Groves School District, and was certainly frequented by Webster Groves book hounds. So as far as I was concerned, it was close enough for this project. In its original location, it was literally a huge old Victorian farmhouse that had hosted a number of businesses before the bookstore, such as a doctor's practice (including a hospital and morgue), a wedding chapel (where ceremonies were sometimes held in the same room that had been the morgue!), an antiques and craft store, a flower shop, and another bookstore before it became home to the family-run bookstore in 1986.

For years, the Book House was one of my favorite haunts.* Each room of the house was dedicated to a different genre or subject, stacked floor to ceiling with books. I can point right now to many books on my bookcases that were surprises and treasures I'd discovered prowling the aisles and combing the shelves of the Book House. I had no idea, though, that in all my visits, not one, not two, but *three* different ghosts may have been prowling those aisles alongside me.

*I apologize ... the pun was right there, and I had to use it.

When owner Michelle Barron first took over the place, it was a true book *house*, she and her family making their home in part of the upstairs while devoting the rest of the building to the bookstore.

I sat down with Michelle in her bookstore. We'd met a few times before over the years, but I'd met a lot fewer bookstore owners than she had bookstore patrons. So after quick reintroductions, she turned the counter over to her staff and retreated with me deeper into the rows of shelves. She led me to a small sitting area where her customers could talk books together or take time to try out a title. The place had that musty, grassy, old-book smell that always marks the best spots to discover paperbound and hardbound treasures. It took only a few moments for us to settle in to our chairs and begin, but as Michelle and I spoke, I have to confess, my attention was more than once diverted from our chat to the titles I occasionally spied over her shoulders as they peeked out from the worn, dark bookcases.

"This goes way back to 1986, and I was in my early twenties," Michelle began. "I was kinda in the midst of a lot of turmoil in my life. My mother—this is relevant—my mother and father had just died within the last couple years. I also had two little children *and* I had just gotten divorced, *and* I was going to school! It was just this crazy time of upheaval."

THE AD THAT STARTED IT

"I was in the midst of looking for a job and looking for another place to live. And I saw this ad in the paper that said 'Bookstore for sale.'

"I had some inheritance money from my father. This friend and I were looking at starting our own business, so I went over there and saw this house. I learned the deal was I could live upstairs, buy all the books this guy had on the lower level—at the time, the books were only two rooms and the first floor had been divided up into stalls for like a little antique mall. But I just loved books and found I could buy all these books for a few thousand dollars and live upstairs and that's all I was thinking at the time. I thought it was something I could do while my kids were little, and then I could always go back to school. So that was the idea. I did also move about thirty boxes of my own collection in there. It was a big junk heap, but slowly, over the years, we got it all together.

"In terms of the ghosts, the first time—literally the minute I walked in the building—I knew I *had* to be there. I had no plan. There was just that ad I randomly saw in the newspaper. I do believe there was some kind of divine intervention. The path I was going wasn't working. I walked in the building and instantly I knew I belonged there. It was overwhelming. I just had to do it, no question.

"So, the first couple nights after we moved in, I had a couple really strange incidents. It was me, a three-year-old, and a six-year-old. One of the first things I did before we could even stay there was install this gate at the top of the stairs, to keep my daughter from falling down the steps. We had this one room we'd kind of blocked off for us to sleep in. We had the kids' beds, and I had a sleeping bag.

"The bathroom had this claw-footed tub. This big, beautiful claw-footed tub. And I decided this was my thing, that I'd light all these candles and soak in the tub. But all the candles kept blowing out! I figured maybe it was just drafty in there.

"So I was lying down, trying to sleep, and I heard the gate I'd put up rattling. And it just kept rattling, like somebody holding it and shaking it *hard!* I thought, 'This really must be some kind of draft!' But I also kept thinking

'Maybe this is my dead mother, coming back to give me some kind of sign.'

"A while later, I had a friend over, and we were talking about it, and my friend just said suddenly, 'I have to leave. There's *something* here, and I have to leave.' He was feeling something really strange. And then I started shaking. Really bad, uncontrollably—to the point I almost went to the emergency room. And I started thinking, 'Maybe this has something to do with my mother.' So I started praying—I didn't know what the heck was going on.

"That night, I was in the sleeping bag, and the shaking with the gate started up again. And then—I can still remember this—I felt this weight, like a heavy blanket, drop on my back. It just enveloped me. You know how you can get so scared you can't move? I knew then something was going on. So I remembered someone telling me once that when weird things like that are happening, visualize a white light.* So I'm thinking 'White light, white light, white light...' and whatever was on my back lifted up and went away.

"After that, I mentioned something to the landlady. I think I actually said, 'This place isn't haunted, is it?' And she said, 'No, nononono ... one of the other ladies here before said something, but *I* never saw anything!' She got really defensive! But at the time, there was no way I was going to be able to move anywhere else, so we were kinda stuck there. We just tried to turn on more lights—that seemed to help.

"We'd see ... *things* ... in the windows upstairs. There was one time, I swear, I saw a face staring in. It was fleeting—I saw it, and then it was gone. I would call the police sometimes, thinking there was somebody in the house. Because of the footsteps and all that, I'd think there

---

Some practitioners of the paranormal maintain that visualizing a white light is a way to protect yourself from negative supernatural energies.

was somebody hiding in there! But the police would come and search. They never found anyone, of course."

Soon, though, they found the activity wasn't limited to the upstairs. Or to the hours of night.

Valerie, the Little Helper

"The store got busier and busier—the business was absolutely fabulous during the day, and it was this amazing place and we were like, 'Wow! I can't believe we're in here!' It was a really beautiful building, with beautiful windows, especially upstairs. One room, the sunset used to shine through its windows, and I had a chair in there ... there was a really *good* feeling about the place. I really felt like I belonged there, that I was supposed to be there. After those initial incidents, it got to feeling like we were accepted. The gate still rattled occasionally and we'd still hear things shuffling around at night—like footsteps. And there was the giggling.

"We used to hear it all the time—employees and customers—giggles, like a kid. And someone running around upstairs when we knew everyone was downstairs. Doors would open and shut.

"I knew some of the previous owners, and they would come in and visit. I met some of the people who grew up there as children. One family, their mom ran a wedding chapel there in the 1960s—I picture it as this *Alice's Restaurant* hippie kind of place. They thought there was something in the house, too, but nothing malevolent. But they did feel there was a spirit in the house.

"I'd been in the house for a year, maybe two, when I met the owner of the old flower shop that used to be in there. The first thing she said to me was 'Have you met Valerie yet?'" Michelle squinted and cocked her head uncertainly, remembering the question. "She went right on, saying, 'Yeah, she's eight years old and walks with a limp.' And I was like 'Okaaayyy...' That did kind of fit with some of the things I had heard, so then we started calling our ghost Valerie.

"Another thing that kept happening was books got moved around a lot. We had a couple of these, like, art books, with dolls on the front—those antique, kinda creepy dolls. I'd go to bed and wake up to find this one laying on the carpet. Then I'd very specifically put it in another place—I'd even show my friend and say, 'Look, I'm putting it right here.' And in the morning, we'd find it back in the little poetry nook, laying on the carpet—the same place every time! I finally handed the book to one of my employees and said, 'Take this book and get it out of here! I can't deal with this!'

"My son has memories of this ghost, too. One of the things that was weird was, when we was between about three and six years old, he had an imaginary friend he would sit up in his room and play with. And he would run around the house pretending to hold somebody's hand all the time. Now, that's kinda normal, so I didn't think much of it. But then we went to go see *Annie* when he was five or six, and he just freaked out! 'I know her!' he kept saying, 'I know her—that's *her!*' Jumping up and down in his seat and practically doing somersaults, he was pointing to the little red-haired girl in the play. 'That's my friend! I play with her all the time!' We went backstage afterwards to talk to the cast—maybe he *had* met her at school or something—but when he met the little actress, he was just embarrassed—it wasn't the girl he thought."

A little red-haired girl he always played with in the house?

"Yes," she nodded slowly.

My research had uncovered accounts of Book House customers seeing a little red-haired girl at the end of a book case, on the stairs, or through a window (even a second-story window!) who sometimes waved and then turned a corner to vanish mysteriously.

She nodded quickly. "Several people do claim that they saw the little red-haired girl in the store."

I'd also read stories of people looking for books in the shop having the exact title they were in search of literally drop suddenly at their feet. There was one account I knew of where a customer claimed she felt a sharp tug on her skirt, from behind her. She turned to discover a book that had just fallen from the shelf—the book she'd come in for. I asked Michelle if those stories were true.

She nodded. "I *witnessed* that happen one time. Someone was looking in the art book section, right there in the front room. She was there for like thirty minutes browsing, wandering back and forth, and then I saw a book fall off the top shelf and land right at her feet. Her face went white and she picked it up and said, 'This is the book I was looking for...' Another time, I had somebody find a book signed by a friend of hers who had just died ... it just fell in her lap.

"We got to the point where we would ask Valerie to help look for stuff. 'Valerie, we can't find this book—could you find it?' Sometimes, it would work!"

Since it was a family-run bookstore, I knew now and then everyone needed to pitch in. I wondered if they ever tried putting Valerie to work, maybe asking her to get a section re-shelved or a set of books boxed. "She was like a kid!" Michelle laughed after considering it, "She wasn't going to do what you wanted her to do!"

She leaned in a bit, wriggling as if her chair was suddenly less comfortable. "One of the creepiest things, the scariest things, I think Valerie did was when I'd be sitting at the desk and I'd feel this *whoosh*," she whipped her hand across her body so her fingers glanced off her opposite shoulder, like she was swatting a fly from her sleeve. "It would literally come and brush up against me like that and move on, like something running past. It was very distinct. I felt that a couple times.

"And I don't know how many times I had customers come up and say, 'I saw something out of the corner of my eye, and I just got freaked out and left.' We'd have customers go upstairs and rush back down, freaked out—that would happen a lot. We'd say 'Valerie, play nice!'— I always talked to her like she was a kid."

THE DARK MAN

Seen less frequently than Valerie, the ghost the Book House staff labelled the Dark Man was far less playful than the little redhead. In fact, he was intimidating. An imposing figure clad all in black, he appeared mostly on the staircases, ether going upstairs or downstairs to the basement.

"Both my family and my customers would see him. My family saw him on the stairs, late at night. Customers saw him in the basement." Michelle let out a slow breath. "The Dark Man, some think, is connected to Valerie. Some of the psychics that came with the investigators said she was afraid of him. Some thought he was maybe someone who abused her in life."

A tall, shadowy figure, what made the Dark Man most eerie to those unfortunate enough to encounter him was the fact he had no face.

"My son would see him. He remembers getting up in the middle of the night to see a dark man with no face. He said the Dark Man would just stand there on the steps and stare. He remembers his bed shaking a lot. He says it used to lift off the floor and shake all the time, and he'd jump off and run to my room to tell me, and he'd see him on the stairs, staring at him. My son would be shaking, he was so scared.

"The customers who saw him said there was this sense of a wall in front of them when he appeared, an invisible barrier you couldn't go through." Some reported browsing in the basement discount section and having the Dark Man block their way when they tried to leave. "He had this scary, cold feeling that was like a wall. The Dark Man, he was something negative."

THE SMOKING MAN

Interestingly, the Book House's third ghost may not have been connected to the house and its history, appearing only after the shop had been open for over fifteen years. Michelle nodded when I asked her about him. "I think the Smoking Man, I think that one we brought in with a book collection.

"People say ghosts follow the things they loved the most in life. So, of course, if you're taking a whole estate ... that year we took in books from *a lot* of estates. We never did that many after that. We don't pick up large estates like that anymore. But there was a guy in Kirkwood we bought a lot of stuff from, like three truckloads."

The Smoking Man was said to appear as a man walking the aisles, smoking a pipe. He was known to turn a corner and vanish when one of the employees of the paper-filled building, familiar with the concept of kindling, would go to ask him to put out his pipe. The smell of smoke he put off was so strong that on more than one occasion, the Book House staff called the fire department.

"There was one time we called the fire department because we all smelled smoke and I was thinking it was an electrical fire in the walls. Three of us could smell it. For like an hour, three of us followed the smoke smell around the house, like 'There it is! Now it's over here! There it is again!' We'd lose the smell, walk around, and find it again someplace else.

"It was moving! From room to room to room. You could smell it in one room and it would go away. And then it would be in another. You could follow it! And it wasn't a burning paper or electrical fire smell—it was a cigar- or pipe-smoke smell. I thought maybe somebody snuck a cigarette in the basement or the bathroom. We didn't know, so we called the police and the fire department. They sent eight fire trucks over! They had to make everybody leave and had all their sensors out. They went through the whole place. And nothing. With all the equipment, they couldn't detect a thing!" She rolled her eyes with a long, amused sigh. "The poor police and firefighters thought we were nuts!

"After that, I think he was walking around here with his pipe, looking at the shelves. I never saw him, but we could smell the pipe smoke. I love the idea that he found a place to stay. He probably lived a good life, passed away, and found a place that was comfortable. Walking around with his pipe, looking at books—the guy was probably in Heaven!"

NOBODY KNOWS THE REAL HISTORY

"The house was a homestead house. It was there before there was any city there—it was already in existence when they *started* keeping records here. The Historical Society had a hard time even dating it. Looking at the structure, they could date some of the boards back two hundred years. But whether the house stood all that time or was built over an older house, they couldn't say. They could only tell us it was built somewhere between 1820 and 1865—there's a record of it being there in 1865 for sure. But we think it predates all that recordkeeping. There were people probably buried on that property in the early days, too.

"The records of the building, of the ownership, are sketchy. A boat captain from New Orleans owned it for a time. It was a boarding house or an inn for some time, and we think a brothel at one point. People came and went. It was also a sheep ranch for a while.

"It became a doctor's office in the 1920s." It was a hospital and morgue, she told me, and people were laid out there regularly. "There was a guy I knew over at the Amoco that remembered his father being laid out there. Then it became a wedding chapel, so go figure. There's a lot that happened there. A lot of people lived a lot of life there, and I think that all became part of the building, part of its energy."

Her eyes sprang wide as she suddenly remembered, "The well was still there! And there's caves, actually caves down under there. Under that part of the city, it's all limestone caves, and water flows under there." For some, that detail is further evidence for supernatural incidents: Many paranormal researchers believe running water can attract and intensify ghost and haunting occurrences, especially when it runs through limestone. They claim such an environment energizes the activity.

A House No More

The Book House, a beloved community favorite and multiple winner of *Best of St. Louis* and *St. Louis A-List* awards, unfortunately no longer stands on its original haunted ground. In 2013, the landmark for St. Louis booklovers was forced to move a new location to make room for construction of a storage facility.

Based on my other interviews, I knew well that the spirits in a building typically don't like change. I was curious how they reacted to the massive undertaking of tens of thousands of books and their fixtures being boxed up and moved.

"When we first moved in, it was like they were testing us out. Then we all got comfortable and it was like they knew we were going to respect them, and everything would be fine. They were okay and everyone lived fine together.

"I tried to leave—several times, I intended to quit, go back to school—but I kept feeling I was being pulled back into that house, like I could never leave it. I could never break away from it. Part of that's the book business." She sank back into her chair, surrendering. "The book business does that to you. You can't ever leave," she chuckled, curling her fingers into claws. "You get trapped into it.

"I really felt like I was meant to be there. One of the theories is that Valerie was a little girl looking for her mother, and I'm the mom of the house, and that's why I felt pulled to be there. Women with red hair have been the owners of the house, going back through seven different women." She listed them all for me starting with herself, the line extending several decades. "Seven red-haired women have been the matriarchs of that house. There's something to that.

"After we moved out, and the place was empty, we did a ghost investigation overnight. We made it our goal to reach that little girl's spirit, to tell her the house was going and wouldn't be there any more, that she needed to move on. We had the investigation team, we invited customers ... we had about twenty-five people in there. We had all the lights off and all this investigation equipment, and it got really spooky really quick! People said they talked to Valerie and saw her—my daughter says she jumped on her back, even! I left about three in the morning... I couldn't handle any more!

"She must've known she had to go. Eight years earlier, when we tried to move out of there, all kinds of crap started happing. Stuff started falling off the shelves all the time, the doors were opening ... there were a lot of noises and a lot of activity. And everything I was trying to do to get away just kept falling through. It just wasn't working. It was like, 'No, you can't leave!' That's usually what happened any time we started stirring things up or tried to do some construction—stuff would start happening.

"But the last time, when we were moving all the books out, we were packing and moving for weeks, and we didn't feel anything. Nothing happened. It was like she was already gone. I don't know... I just didn't feel it. I went back in there when the place was completely vacant. I just didn't feel it. Something was missing. I think she did move on. We were *all* ready to move on!"

BOOKS ARE ORGANIC OBJECTS

Even with the all investigators she had in the old place through the years, each with their own ideas for the causes of the activity, Michelle has her own theories about the goings-on in the old Book House. "Books are organic objects," she explained, "and they hold connections. As soon as you touch something, it changes. Two objects that touch become connected.

"My theory is that books are time-travelling objects, like a portkey in Harry Potter.* Old books and old objects, I think, hold energy in a way I think people in the modern, disposable world aren't used to anymore." She plucked a handful of old titles from a nearby shelf, weighing them in her hand. "So, I think, bringing together an old, old house like that with all the old books created an energy and environment that attracted these things. I think people today aren't used to old things and how they feel. People just don't understand how objects hold history—and they do hold history. Physics, quantum physics, shows how

---

*In J.K. Rowling's *Harry Potter* books, a portkey is a magic object that, when touched, transports whoever touched it to a particular place.

atoms and particles interact and create change in one another. And they stay connected."

ONE FINAL QUESTION

The new location for the bookstore, where we sat talking, was just a couple miles up the road from the original location. Just as idiosyncratic a building as the first, the new Book House takes up two floors of what was once an old department store. So the question to me now is: Did the ghosts follow the books to a new home?

"No!" Michelle exclaimed, disappointment plain in her voice. Then she laughed, "Some people, that's the only reason they came in! This place isn't haunted." She shook her head. "We keep looking for it to be haunted. We *wish* it was haunted."

Atalanta Avenue

"It took me a few years to realize that there was something going on in the house," D—— told me once we sat down together. I'd been put in contact with her by another homeowner I'd interviewed. She'd told me of a friend of hers who had also experienced the unexplained in a Webster Groves home. With both of us in busy, conflicting schedules, D—— and I had a few hits and misses in getting together to talk. But at last, I was able to sit down for a few minutes in person with her.

D—— was very focused as we spoke, her eyes holding steady on mine as she recounted the happenings in her home. "This isn't the kind of story that really starts at a beginning or has particular incidents that are really wild or anything like that, so it's kind of *interesting*.

"In a few months, it'll be twenty years that I've been living on Atalanta. The house is two stories, an old farmhouse built in 1897. One thing I've learned is that it had a lot of owners who didn't know what they were doing fixing up the house, so I have a love/hate relationship with this interesting old home."

As an owner of an old Webster Groves home myself, I commiserated with her on that.

"I always felt the house, because it had been neglected and unfixed, felt unloved ... if a house can feel anything. After two or three years living there, I had a change of circumstances, with my husband moving out and my boyfriend moving in. That was when things really started to act up in the house."

Noises, The Little Girl Upstairs, and
Peter Pan in the Basement

"Up until then, I was getting used to the noises of an old home: the way the furnace was so noisy, the way the windows rattled, the way the floorboards in the stairs creaked—all of that. I attributed any unusual noises to that kind of thing.

"But the things that had been going on in the house had made me suspicious that there could be *something* there ... and I always had the feeling it was a child, a girl.

"One of the noises that I would hear was a single note on the piano. It was a *note* I could duplicate, but I could never duplicate the *way* that it was pressed, how *lightly* it was pressed. It was always just a single note. It reminded me of what kids do with a piano—they come and they just touch one key.

"I never saw anything. I would hear noises in various parts of the house when no one was there. I had people who would come over for parties who asked me questions about noises in the house. They'd be in the back area and hear noises upstairs. Footsteps—" she clarified, "—it was always footsteps and floor creaks, like someone slowly putting their weight on a floor board. I would go and look and there'd be nobody else in the house.

"Then one day, I was up in my bedroom, in front of my mirror. I was standing there, getting ready, and I felt a tug. It was like a child tugging on the lower part of my shirt. I looked in the mirror, and I could see my shirt pulling, the wrinkles in the fabric going taut. I was looking in the mirror and saw there was nothing behind me. Then I looked over my shoulder to be sure. There was *nothing* behind me!

"Even with the tugging on the shirt, still, I wasn't convinced. I didn't want to think—didn't want to really believe."

The tugging on the shirt would have convinced me, I assured her.

"I was a skeptic," she shrugged. "I *wanted* to be a skeptic."

"About two to three weeks later, my boyfriend was in the kitchen making dinner. He had two young daughters, the youngest of which, T——, was eight. The girls were over that night, watching TV in the back room. I came into the kitchen. I could tell he was a little freaked out and he said, 'Something just happened that was really weird: I was standing here at the sink, and I felt, like, a kid tug at the back of my shirt. I figured it was T—— and I turned around ... and nobody was there!'

"'Oh my God!' I blurted, 'I had the same thing happen upstairs. I thought for sure it was a kid tugging on the back of *my* shirt!' Then he started telling me stories and said, 'There's this note on the piano...' Now, he was a musician and had perfect pitch. He walked over to the piano and hit the key and that was it—the note I'd been hearing.

"After that, we noticed more and more. He told me about a situation that happened in the basement where he saw a figure of a person. It was small and dark and flat, like a shadow. 'Boylike,' he described, 'like Peter Pan.' He saw it go across the basement—not against the wall, but across the middle of the room—and then it went *through* him. It felt electrical, he said, and cold. He told me that he just turned then and headed back up the steps and called out 'Hey, we're all friends here. Everything's cool!'" D—— laughed recalling his reaction. Her smile faded. "But he said the whole thing was just eerie.

"People would come over to my house, and in the living room/foyer area—the foyer is where the piano is located—they would talk about the energy of the room, and how it would make them feel really relaxed and calm. That was always the feeling I got from the house. I attribute that to the spirit there being very friendly. I have friends who are very *aware* when it comes to those things—one's a healing psychic—and they have all told me, 'There's more than one here.' So, the Peter Pan-like figure in the basement may not be the same one pulling on clothing."

A Visitor from the Past

"About five years ago, the prior owner of the home—the person I bought it from—showed up at my back door."

The *back* door?

D—— nodded slowly, the *can you believe it?* plain in her expression. "She pulled up in my driveway. It had been over ten years I'd been in the home. She knocked on the back door, not the front door, and when I answered it she asked, 'Do you remember me?'

"I remembered her." D—— squinted. "Let's just say the sale was a little *weird.*

"She said, 'Could I come in and see your house?'

"I thought it was a little odd, and there'd been things done in the home, carpet pulled up and floors put down and such. So I was going through with her, pointing things out, and she beelined right to the foyer."

Where the piano that plays one note all on its own is...

"Yes. She just stood there. She looked into the living room and looked up the steps and finally said, 'This is it. I still dream about these rooms.'

"I said, 'Really...' and then I added, 'The house certainly does have an interesting energy.'

"She turned around and gave me this stare and said, 'What do you mean?'

"I didn't feel comfortable with her, so I simply repeated, 'It just has an interesting energy.' And she left.

"That was all the conversation we had. So, I don't know what she experienced in the home. That was very odd. I could tell she wanted me to say something more, but it just didn't feel *right.*"

Skeptics and Believers

"I have an elderly neighbor who's lived there forever," D——— began, "She's told me, interestingly enough, that going back something like forty years, each person who's sold and moved out of the house left because of a divorce. When my first husband and I divorced, I almost had to move out, for financial reasons."

She didn't hesitate in her story, but I noticed D———'s eyes brighten as a smile tugged at the corners of her mouth and lit her face.

"Last summer, I got married again."

Congratulations.

"Thank you." Keeping the focus she'd demonstrated so far, D——— was right back to recounting her story. "My husband had moved in the year before our wedding. I told him the stories. He's not so much of a skeptic as I was. After he'd been there about six months or so, one night in bed he was awakened out of a sound sleep by a push against his right shoulder. He said he woke up and looked over and I was way on the other side of the bed so he knew it wasn't me that pushed him. And at that moment, he said, 'I know these stories are true.' Whoever this is wanted to let him know 'I know you're here, and you should know I'm here.'

"As different people have been though the house, others have told me of things they've experienced, touches and sensations of things going through them, things like that.

"Now, with all that, my son does not believe. At all. Although he's told me stories that make me think that he's seen things that he just won't admit to. He has also seen shadows at times—but of course, he doesn't believe, so it's kind of a 'whatever' thing for him.

"Just a few weeks ago, he had his girlfriend and her family to the house for dinner. We got to telling stories about the occurrences and my son talked about a dream he had, about this young girl in the home. But it wasn't current—it was in the past. And it was a young African-American girl, which is an interesting thought, with Webster's history.* He said the dream had to do with her being upstairs and then her coming down the steps.

"I asked him, 'When did this happen?' 'Oh it was a *long* time ago,' he replied. 'You've never said anything...' 'Why would I?' he answered, 'It was just a dream.'

"He tells me he doesn't believe. But I believe he's experienced things that fit, in spite of himself." D—— laughed, "I tell him he doesn't *have to* believe."

WHERE THE SKEPTICISM FIRST CRACKED

"Now I'm going to tell you another story, about what got me over my *total* skepticism." D—— brought her hand to her face, resting her chin on her knuckles. She broke eye contact for the first time, her gaze shifting up as she recalled, "I used to live in Soulard.** And Soulard, of course, has many haunting-types of things. We were renting a townhouse sort of building. My husband and I slept on the top floor, my son, who was just a baby, slept on the second floor, and there was living space on the first. When my son was about three years old, he said to me, 'Mama, who is that lady?'

"I had never told anybody about the lady." D—— explained. "I woke up one night in my bedroom, and it was very dark and there was a figure of a turn-of-the-century woman, hair pulled back, with a high-collared long dress. She was young, beautiful. She was transparent in her upper part, and just sort of disappeared as she got lower down into her dress—nothing in her lower part. I wondered if

*After the Civil War, many black families settled in Webster Groves; During segregation, Webster Groves was home to Douglass High School, for decades the only accredited high school for blacks in all of St. Louis County.

**One of the oldest neighborhoods in the City of St. Louis.

I was dreaming as I watched her come around the room and go down the steps and then disappear. I saw her again a few months after that, in similar circumstances.

"So when my son said to me, 'Who's that lady?' I said 'What lady?' 'She's old-fashioned-looking,' he told me, 'and has her hair up.' I asked him, 'What do you mean, *old-fashioned-looking?*' Now, he was a very verbal three-year-old and he said 'She had old clothes, you know, like clothes from a hundred years ago.' I said, 'Really?' 'Yes,' he declared, 'I saw her.'

"I said, 'Honestly, I don't know who she is, but I've seen her too.'

"Of course, his father said, 'You guys are crazy. And you shouldn't be filling this child's head with these things.'

"That was when I first came to the point where my skepticism wavered and I thought, 'There's something to this.'"

Still Happening?

I'd noticed D—— spoke of the activity in her home in terms of others' experiences—her husband's, her boyfriend's, her party guests', her son's—and I asked if she still encountered the little girl upstairs or Peter Pan in the basement.

"I don't experience activity anymore. It's others who experience it now. It's almost like the spirit and I have come to terms. We live side-by-side and we're perfectly okay with that. So there's no reason to prove anything to me. Of course, that's just my mind —what do I know?

"It's other people who seem to continue to experience things. My husband told me—and this is just in the last week—he was in the bedroom alone one day during the daytime. No one was home. He said he heard a creak on the steps—our top step creaks whenever anyone puts any weight on it. He said it sounded like someone right outside the room putting a foot down slowly on the creaky board and then *slooowly* letting it back up. He said he opened the bedroom door, and of course, no one was there.

"So he's the one experiencing most of the noises. He's commented on the piano key—he said to me, 'There's a particular key on the piano...' I asked him where he is when he's heard it. I've always been in the kitchen or the dining room when I've heard it, or upstairs—no place close to the foyer. He told me he's been in the living room watching TV when it's happened, adjacent to the foyer and the piano! He said he looks over and the piano's right there, with no one around it.

"I don't know why this particular spirit hangs around. I can't help her transition to the other side. I was already aware of things by the time I moved into the house on Atalanta. I think that's why my experience there has been different than my first—this time, I didn't have to *see* to believe."

Tuxedo Boulevard

I met K—— working together on the annual PTO plays at the grade school our kids both attended. I'd known her for years, and was surprised to learn she had her own story of a haunting in her home. We sat down to talk on a Friday evening. Coughing peppered her conversation as we started. "Allergies," she apologized.

"Just to give you a little background," she began soberly, "I come from a long line of women who are clairvoyant or have other gifts. My mom told me it skipped a generation with her. But she told me the stories my whole life. I didn't want any part in it, didn't want to believe it. Until I started having experiences of my own.

"Our house was built in 1923. It was a small, old-style bungalow. We moved in, just me and my husband at the time. I'd never had an experience with anything supernatural or metaphysical before...

"Within maybe a month, it started. I would get up in the middle of the night to go to the bathroom. I'd head back to the bedroom, and as soon as I had my back to the dining room, I'd get the heebie-jeebies, like a tickling up my spine. Not like someone touching me, but a tingling—you know that feeling like someone's watching you? I would turn and look, but it was dark in the dining room so, of course, I couldn't see anything. I always got this funny feeling, and it was always from the same area of the room.

"Over time, I noticed it more and more at night. And then, when I was home during the day, I started to see something."

The Shape

"It was dark and low to the ground, football-shaped and actually about the size of a football. I'd see it out of the corner of my eye, and when I'd turn and look, there would be nothing there. So I'd think. 'Okay, maybe I looked into the sun or some bright light'—you make a lot of excuses, you know? And you don't want to think you're crazy. That's why I didn't tell my husband—he was an engineer, and would have been ready at that point to put me in a straightjacket.

"I couldn't really believe what I was seeing, either. But over time—I'm thinking it was eight months to a year— that shape slowly changed. At first, it rotated so it was upright on one end instead of laying flat."

Like for a place-kick, I offered.

"Yes. And the more I noticed it, the more I *noticed* it. I only saw it in the dining room, and always out of the corner of my eye. Over that time, it stretched and grew, elongating until it was slightly taller than me and shaped ... like a baguette. And every time I'd turn to look straight on at it, nothing was there. It kept happening, a couple times a week, mostly at night. And then it was daily, night and day, for almost a year." K—— began coughing again. A sip of coffee quieted the tickle in her throat, and she went to refresh her cup before continuing.

"I started to think about it more." K—— said as she settled into her chair again. "The more I thought about it, the more I realized I had feelings about it. And I started to have a feeling that it was a human being's spirit. I had never believed in that kind of thing. I thought it was absolutely hocus-pocus, despite the stories my mom used to tell me as a kid—I thought all those people were crazy. So I didn't tell anybody at all. No one. Because I just thought that no one would believe me, that they'd say I was seeing things.

"But I also started to feel like there was something wrong with the Shape, about three-quarters of the way up, like in what would be its chest. Like its heart. And I felt now it was male.

"Time went by, maybe another half year or more, and I finally told it all to a girl from work, because she was completely dissociated from my personal life and also because she had told me about an experience she'd had—like someone blowing on her while she was doing dishes, kissing the back of her neck and stuff like that. So I felt safe telling her.

"She said, 'You know, I read up on this because it was bothering me so much at my house. Sometimes, a spirit is trapped between two worlds for some reason. They're still holding on to their human life, and sometimes, if you just talk to it and tell it to go, it will.'

"'That's crazy,' I thought, 'I'm not talking to a baguette!'" K—— laughed. "'Or a football!'" The smile faded from her face. "Then I started to notice it in other parts of the house. But still only out of the corner of my eye. Every time I turned to look, *poof!* it was gone.

"I had this feeling now that it wanted to appear to me. I was never scared of it. I'd get the heebie-jeebies and be creeped out, but it never *scared* me. Nothing ever moved on its own in the house, and I never felt I was having tricks played on me, never felt anything evil was happening. It was just observation after observation. And I felt like I was being watched.

"Now, that house had a beautiful and well-maintained garden of perennials. I studied horticulture in college and I could tell somebody had really loved that yard, really appreciated it and took good care of it.

"I came home one night after a cross-country drive to return from a wedding. One of the other bridesmaids was a friend and had driven with me.

She came in to help drop off my bags and asked, 'Can we take a walk?'

"I said, 'Sure.' So we headed up Tuxedo and got about half-way to the next street when she said, 'I don't want to freak you out or anything, but there's *something* in your house...' As soon as she said it, I knew what she meant. She could have been saying there were mice in the house or ants, but I knew she was talking about the Shape.

" 'I've had experiences like this,' she told me. 'Not that I ever want to. But I'll walk into somebody's house sometimes, and I'll see or feel something. And I felt something in your house.'

" 'That's very interesting,' I said to her, 'because I've been having this experience over the last almost two years.' I told her a little more, and she told me the same thing the girl from work told me: that it was something caught between the two worlds. 'For some reason,' she said to me, 'it's choosing to appear to you like this. It doesn't want to scare you, which is why it disappears when you look directly at it. That's why it's not doing anything to you ... moving stuff or making sounds. It doesn't mean to bother you. It's just ... hangin' out.'

"And then she told me, 'Sometimes, if somebody's really connected to a place, then something about their spirit stays and remains there. Whether it's unfinished business or a place that they really loved or someplace where they were terrorized, or if they just can't let go because they feel they haven't forgiven...'" I noticed K——'s voice tightening. " 'Whatever the reason, that soul is still connected to that place. And sometimes, you just need to help them along.'

"Right," K—— rolled her eyes recalling it, shaking her head. "Again, it was like, 'I'm not talking to the baguette!' I couldn't picture myself talking to thin air. It was silly.

"So more time went by, maybe another six months. I was seeing this thing out of the corner of my eye all the time. I knew it was male, and I knew there was something wrong with his chest. And by feeling, by intuition, I knew this spirit was just hangin' out. But I didn't know why, and that was bothering me because I was sharing this space—my home—with somebody who wasn't invited. And on top of that, part of me felt the problem was that I needed *him* to invite *me* to *his* space.

The Neighbor Holds the Answers

"One day, I was talking to my eighty-four year old neighbor from across the street. He used to work at the Webster Groves Library for years, taking care of the landscaping. He'd lived in that house for a long, long, *long* time.

"It was a summer day, and we were working in our yards. We were talking about yards and landscaping. Just small talk, shootin' the breeze. And I said, 'Somebody must have really loved my yard at some point, loved the plants and really appreciated the place.'

"'Oh, yeah,' my neighbor said, 'Mr. and Mrs. G——. They came here from Germany, to flee World War II.'

"Now, I knew that name. Ever since moving into the house, we'd been getting mail—junk mail—for not the previous owner who we bought the house from, but the owner before that: Mr. G——.

"My neighbor told me how, under Hitler and the Nazis, Mr. G—— had been held and experimented on. They did biological testing, and the man ultimately died of breast cancer, induced by what they did to him.

"That was it. My friend the baguette, the Shape ... it was Mr. G——: a man, with something wrong with his chest; who fled the evil of Hitler's regime and appreciated the sanctuary he'd found here in the United States of America; the person whose mail I'd been getting for two years—still connected to the home he and his wife loved and cherished and worked hard on, as you could see in the yard, *still connected to the property.*

"I didn't say anything to my neighbor—what would I say? 'Oh, yeah, Mr. G——you're talking about the baguette in my dining room. Yep, he's still hangin' around.'

"When he told me that, I knew that's who it was. But I still wasn't ready to encounter or talk to or interact with it, whatever it was, exactly.

"It wasn't until one day doing housework, that I had my only physical encounter with it. It was just like they always describe: a sensation like a cold wind passing through you. It stopped me dead in my tracks. I wish I had a video of myself so I could see if my hair blew—it felt that real and strong."

L—— coughed and cleared her throat. "I didn't have anything planned to say. I had never planned anything to say. But I went into this talk, this monologue: 'I know that you loved this house. And I know you felt safe here in Webster Groves. I know this was a home and community that you loved, that it was a sanctuary from all the horrors you faced, and that you're still connected to it all. But I'm going to take really good care of your house. It's safe, and it's in good hands. You can go now if you want to. You don't have to take care of this place anymore, and you can go and be at peace.'

"That was the last day I saw my baguette." Her voice was smaller, and she forced a slight smile. K—— settled back in her chair, drained, her eyes glistening. "I've got goosebumps," she said.

So did I.

Afterword

I've always been interested in the mysterious and the unexplained. I was a kid with a big imagination fed on comic books, science fiction novels, cartoons, mythology, movies, *Star Trek* ... adventure, mystery, and the unknown were the blocks that made up the world for me.

When I was in second grade, I remember finding a book in my elementary school library, *Haunted Houses* by Larry Kettelkamp. It was a small nonfiction book that purported to explain and detail hauntings and ghostly activity from an investigative point of view. Its cover featured the famous Tulip Staircase photo, and inside were more pictures of the unquiet dead, such as the famous Brown Lady of Raynham Hall, all captured in black-and-white as supposed photographic proof of their existence.

I couldn't tell you how many times I checked that book out that year, or how many more times I checked it out in the years of elementary school that followed. It fascinated me, and sparked a lifelong interest that resulted in the book you hold in your hands right now.

Are ghosts real? I don't know. Science can't explain them ... but then again, science can't explain a lot of things until it *can* explain them. But as the firsthand accounts in this book show, many people—even in as relatively small an area as Webster Groves—have experienced something they can't explain yet understand as an encounter with a ghost. The patterns and similarities among the stories are striking: the sense of being tested that some reported; apparitions choosing staircases to materialize upon; children's imaginary friends that perhaps aren't so imaginary, adults feeling a responsibility to spirits they perceive as children's; the faceless visions; and the way change—moving in, moving out, renovating—seems to stir up activity.

The people I interviewed ... these are their stories. I can find no reason to discount them. And as a storyteller, I can find plenty of reasons to accept them as told. Author Yan Martel said once, explaining his award-winning novel *Life of Pi*, "Life is a story. You can choose your story. A story with God is the better story."

I would express the same sentiment about ghosts.

So, for the last tale in this collection, I have one more unexplained experience in an old Webster Groves house to recount.

My own.

Not long after getting married, we bought a home in Webster Groves. An English-style cottage, it was just that size that's a little big for two, a little crowded with children, and then somehow empty without them. We'd been living there a couple years, just my wife and me, a family still another year or two down the road for us. Our schedules were a little offset, and most days she would leave for work before I was even out of bed. Some mornings she would wake me before she left, to say goodbye.

On one morning, I remember waking near sunrise. Squinting at the clock, I rolled over to doze a few more minutes before the alarm sounded. I was surprised when I felt someone sit down on the bed, the mattress sinking behind me—I hadn't heard my wife enter our room. I waited there, expecting a hand on my shoulder to nudge me awake or a whispered "Goodbye. See you tonight." Neither came, puzzling me. I was about to turn over.

And then I heard my wife on the stairs.

Like almost every Webster Groves house, ours was several decades old—that's part of the area's charm. Its walls creaked and rasped, settling as the seasons changed.

The old stairs from the first floor, which ended right outside our bedroom door, always groaned whenever anyone was on them.

Unmistakably, someone was coming up the stairs.

Confused, I then heard the bedroom door open, light from the hall starting to spill in. I felt the weight behind me jump from the bed, the mattress levelling again beside me. I rolled over to see my wife in the doorway, her hand still on the doorknob as she leaned in from the hall. "Bye," she whispered with a smile.

My eyes darted over the darkened room. There was, of course, no one else there.

In all the years since, I've wakened to that weight behind me on the bed only a handful of times more, perhaps three or four. I never saw anything when I felt the mattress suddenly slope and I never again felt it jump up off the bed. At this point, it's been easily ten years since the last time it happened.

Now, for the skeptics: I will completely concede that all those subsequent times, I could have been dreaming. The sensation of the weight on the bed could have been some exercise of my unconscious imagination in the gray mental twilight of an episode of *in somnis oppressus* or hypnopompic sleep paralysis.

But not that first time. When I heard my wife on the steps, when the door opened, when I felt the weight spring from the bed ... with no doubt, *I was wide awake.*

Was it a ghost? I don't know. But a story with a ghost is a better story.

Thanks

I owe special thanks to everyone who was good enough to share their stories with me. I learned quickly that for some these were very personal experiences for their families, and I appreciate the trust they put in me to share them appropriately.

But as many people told me their stories, many more put me in contact with those who had stories or pointed me to information that led to the interviews here. A book like this doesn't happen on its own, so thanks to everyone who helped me in unearthing and collecting these stories of the ghosts and hauntings in the neighborhoods of my community, Webster Groves: Amelia Dorsey, Anna Dorsey, Billy Ratz, Brian Ackley, Brian Rohlfing, Debbie Love, Katie Puglisi, Jim Longo, Lori Callander, Michelle Barron, Nessa Dorsey, Peter Sargent, Richard Hibbs, The St. Louis Repertory Theatre, The Theatre Guild of Webster Groves, and Webster University.

References

"A Short History of Webster University." *Webster University*. Webster University, n.d. Web. 29 May 2015. <http://www.webster.edu/faculty/faculty_resource_guide/welcome/history.html>.

"About The Rep." *The Repertory Theatre of St. Louis: History of the Rep*. The Repertory Theatre of St. Louis, n.d. Web. 26 May 2015. <http://www.repstl.org/history/>.

"About Us." *The Book House*. The Book House, Inc., n.d. Web. 08 July 2015. <http://www.bookhousestl.com/?page=shop/aboutus>.

"Area History." *Webster Groves, Missouri*. City of Webster Groves, n.d. Web. 04 May 2015. <http://www.webstergroves.org/index.aspx?nid=137>

"Area History." *Webster Groves/Shrewsbury/Rock Hill Area Chamber of Commerce*. WGSRH Chamber, n.d. Web. 04 May 2015. <http://www.go-webster.com/history.htm>.

Brown, Alan. *Ghosts Along the Mississippi River*. Jackson: U of Mississippi, 2011. Print.

Courtaway, Robbi. *Spirits of St. Louis: A Ghostly Guide to the Mound City's Unearthly Activities*. St. Louis, MO: Virginia Pub., 1999. Print.

Courtaway, Robbi. *Spirits of St. Louis II: Return of the Gateway City Ghosts*. St. Louis, MO: Virginia Pub., 2002. Print.

Demariano, A. "Ghost Stories from Maria Hall." *YouTube*. YouTube, 1 Nov. 2011. Web. 14 June 2015.

Demariano, A. "The Ghost That Haunts Webster
University's Loretto Hall." *Webster Journal Online.*
Webster University, 31 Oct. 2011. Web. 14 June 2015.

Franzen, Jonathan. *The Discomfort Zone: A Personal History.*
New York: Farrar, Straus and Giroux, 2006. Print.

"Ghost Hunting? Here's Where You May Find Some
Spirits of St. Louis." *STLToday.com.* St. Louis
Post-Dispatch, 24 Oct. 2014. Web. 29 June 2015.
<http://www.stltoday.com/entertainment/ghost-
hunting-here-s-where-you-may-find-some-spirits/
article_51e6f9f1-2717-5069-badc-f3faf4c7b910.html>.

Gibbs, Nancy. "A Week in the Life of a High School." *Time*
25 Oct. 1999: 67-103. Web. 21 May 2015.

Gilbert, Joan. *Missouri Ghosts.* 2nd Edition. Hallsville, MO:
MoGho Books, 2001. Print.

Hauck, Dennis William. *Haunted Places: The National
Directory.* NY: Penguin Books, 1996. Print.

"History." *Great Circle.* Great Circle, n.d. Web. 25 June 2015.
<https://www.greatcircle.org/about/history.html>.

"History of the Seminary." *Kenrick-Glennon Seminary.*
Kenrick-Glennon Seminary, n.d. Web. 13 July 2015.
<http://www.kenrick.edu/about/history-of-kenrick-
glennon-seminary/>.

Holzer, Hans. *Ghosts: True Encounters with the World Beyond.*
NY: Black Dog & Leventhal Publishers, Inc., 1997. Print.

Kettelkamp, Larry. *Haunted Houses.* New York:
Morrow, 1969. Print.

Leslie, Mark. *Tomes of Terror: Haunted Bookstores and
Libraries.* Toronto: Dundurn, 2014. Print.

Longo, Jim. *Haunted Odyssey: Ghostly Tales of the Mississippi Valley*. St. Louis. MO: Ste. Anne's Press, 1986. Print.

Renton, Jennie. "Yann Martel Interview." *Textualities*. Main Point Books, 2005. Web. 01 June 2015. <http://textualities.net/jennie-renton/yann-martel-interview>.

Shanks, Holly. "Webster Theatre a Landmark of Webster History." *Webster Journal Online*. Webster University, 13 Nov. 2013. Web. 15 May 2015.

Shapiro, Mary. "Theatre Guild of Webster Groves Up for Landmark Designation." *Webster-Kirkwood Times* 25 Oct 2013. Web. 13 May 2015.

Shortridge, Julie. "The Book House." *Haunted Missouri*. Blogspot.com, 24 Jan. 2009. Web. 08 July 2015. <http://hauntedmissouri.blogspot.com/2009/01/book-house.html>.

Taylor, Troy. *Haunted St. Louis: History & Hauntings Along the Mississippi*. Alton, IL: Whitechapel Productions, 2002. Print.

Yohe, Timothy. "The Book House: A Tale of a Haunting." *Paranormal Insights*. Blogspot.com, 13 June 2015. Web. 10 July 2015. <http://ghosttracker423.blogspot.com/2015/06/the-book-house-tale-of-haunting.html>.

Thanks for reading this Factual Planet Chronicle. Knowledge unshared is knowledge lost, so if you loved this book, be sure to share it with your friends and followers or post a short review with your favorite bookseller or forum!

About the Author

Patrick Dorsey has been a natural storyteller his whole life, beginning in first grade when he started stapling together crayoned pages to make his own books. He's the author of the international hit Knights Templar adventure *God's Forge* (his first book published without a stapler or crayons) and the upcoming novel *The Champion Sky*, both from Legendary Planet.

Following a lifelong fascination with the mysterious and the unknown, he began researching his community and interviewing friends and neighbors to collect the eerie firsthand accounts that became *Haunted Webster Groves*.

Also of Interest from Factual Planet and Legendary Planet

An Authenticated History of the Famous Bell Witch, the Wonder of the 19th Century and Unexplained Phenomenon of the Christian Era
by Martin Van Buren Ingram

Candle Game:™ Kaidankai
(featuring weird and ghostly tales of Old Japan by Lafcadio Hearn)

Candle Game:™ Ghost Stories of an Antiquary
(featuring ghostly stories by M.R. James)

Do you have a ghostly experience in either the
Webster Groves, Missouri or Kirkwood, Missouri
areas that you'd like to share? Email your contact
information to *Ghosts@LegendaryPlanet.com*

Made in the USA
San Bernardino, CA
14 January 2016